Don't Plant Your Seeds Among Thorns

A Catholic's Guide to Recognizing
and Healing from Domestic Abuse

Jenny duBay

En Route Books and Media, LLC
Saint Louis, MO

⊕*ENROUTE*
Make the time

En Route Books and Media, LLC
5705 Rhodes Avenue
St. Louis, MO 63109

Cover credit: Sebastian Mahfood

ISBN-13: 979-8-88870-169-0
Library of Congress Control Number:
Available at https://catalog.loc.gov

"In ministry, I encounter women daily who are living in marriages characterized by manipulation, blame, coercion, denial and other forms of violence – emotional and spiritual as well as physical or sexual violence. These abusive experiences are a profound violation of our human dignity! Intimate partner violence leaves women feeling confused, alone, filled with despair and even suicidal. I am grateful to Jenny duBay for writing this book. With a solidly Catholic voice, Jenny addresses the oft-underemphasized reality of domestic violence and spousal abuse within Catholic marriages. The truth, clarity and practical advice contained in this book make it an invaluable resource for those enduring such trauma, and for those of us walking alongside of God's wounded daughters." – **De Yarrison, CPCC, foundress of You Are Made New Ministry and Laura Ercolino, foundress of Hope's Garden**

"Jenny duBay's *Don't Plant Your Seeds Among Thorns: A Catholic's Guide to Recognizing and Healing from Domestic Abuse* is not simply a book, but a lifeline for those seeking healing, understanding, and hope in the context of the Catholic Faith. Throughout this work the author's wisdom and empathy shine through each page, which results in the illumination of a definitive path towards the reclaiming of one's dignity and becoming a survivor of abuse, especially abuse within the institution of marriage." – **Christina M. Sorrentino, author of Belonging to Christ: Catholic Poetry and contributor to Missio Dei's book, The Eucharistic Revival Project**

"Should Catholics stay in an abusive relationship? Jenny duBay answers this question with such clarity and heart in her book *Don't Plant Your Seeds Among Thorns*. Comprehensive, practical and healing, this book is a must-read for anyone suffering from an abusive relationship. Coming from an expert and survivor of domestic abuse, the author will guide you as you seek to understand, forgive, move on and heal from the trauma of abuse. There is hope and healing even when all else seems lost." – **Jocelyn Soriano, author of various self-help and Catholic books including Mend My Broken Heart and 366 Days of Compassion, book reviewer, and writer of the Patheos column "Beloved"**

"Jenny duBay is an author who writes with a deep understanding of God's mercy, through which she hopes to communicate God's love to others. She has a particular calling to provide healing to those who have suffered from domestic violence, and a desire to provide hope to those who feel forsaken. For any who are seeking inspiration or direction from the brokenness of life, I whole-heartedly endorse her writings. In her word's, God's love is waiting for you." – **Michael Snellen, founder of I AM Catholic and Catholic Creators**

What Others Say about *Don't Plant Your Seeds Among Thorns*

"The Catechism observes that God's original plan for marriage has been 'seriously disturbed' by sin (1608). As a result, man and woman's 'mutual attraction, the Creator's own gift, changed into a relationship of domination and lust' (1607). In *Don't Plant Your Seeds Among Thorns: A Catholic's Guide to Recognizing and Healing from Domestic Abuse*, Jenny duBay compassionately discusses the true nature of marriage while providing resources and hope for those who aren't experiencing authentic companionship in their relationships. Drawing from the Catechism, the Theology of the Body, and various other trusted Catholic resources, Jenny opens the way to genuine healing for those seeking freedom from abusive relationships." **– Christopher West, Th.D., best-selling author, popular podcaster, and President, Theology of the Body Institute**

"Jenny duBay has written a marvelous book, *Don't Plant Your Seeds Among the Thorns*, that covers the topic of intimate partner abuse thoroughly and sensitively. As a survivor herself, she understands its deceitful trap, its traumatic impact as well as the courageous steps necessary to escape it. Significantly, her book addresses the problem from the point of view of the Christian faith. Jenny duBay plumbs the meaning of scripture and helps victims and survivors connect their faith with the evil they have experienced. She emphasizes the need for spiritual healing and guides the wounded along pathways to a new and regenerated life. Her book should be required reading for all parish ministers." **– Fr. Charles W. Dahm, O.P., Director of Archdiocese of Chicago Domestic Violence Outreach, from the "Foreword"**

"Jenny duBay has created a tender wake-up call for wounded wives in abusive marriages. She brilliantly blends Holy scripture and church teachings with the truth around abuse in marriage. Her candid psychoeducation is balanced with gentle, directed encouragement toward spiritual truths that wives need to understand because so often misinformed church leaders and culture are teaching the opposite. She doesn't skirt around the toughest of issues – sexual violence in marriage. Jenny's heart for women to find their assertive spirit through Jesus and find empowerment to make choices based on safety is very clear. I highly recommend this book to any Catholic woman who is struggling to make sense of a confusing marriage." – **Bonny Logsdon Burns, Certified Partner Coach through the Association of Partners of Sex Addicts Trauma Specialists and co-host of Hope for Wives podcast.**

"With candor and conciseness, Jenny duBay has written a book that brings clarity and practical wisdom for men and women who may find themselves stuck in the suffocating cycle of domestic abuse. I am certain that this compendium of insight into abuse, the Church's teachings on marriage, and steps to escape such physical and mental violence will assist many in pursuing the respite they desperately need and in a manner that corresponds with the Church's long-standing wisdom." - **Angela Erickson, host of the Integrated with Angela podcast**

"In a caring and heartfelt manner, Jenny duBay has gifted us with a comprehensive book about intimate partner violence, from a Catholic perspective. She provides practical information and describes ways to recognize an unhealthy relationship and journey to a space of hope and healing for all harmed or who cause harm in this way. Also, it is a must-read for all those accompanying people on their path to live a safe and sacred life free of violence." – **Sharon O'Brien, Ph.D., Co-Founder and Executive Director of Catholics for Family Peace, Initiative of National Institute for the Family**

Dedication

To my children, Takoda and Keariel Peasley, who have been incredibly understanding and patient with me throughout this entire journey and have also been continual sources of unconditional love.

My mother: To my mother, Kathy Daley—who has been a fount of advice, maternal care, and support.

Finally, *to my brother*, Dave DuBay, who made sure I was safe both physically and emotionally during my roughest years, and who has always been there for me when needed. I knew I could turn to him in any emergency, and although that never happened, just the knowledge of such support was balm to my soul.

Thank you, all. From the depths of my newly-awakened soul.

Acknowledgments

First and foremost, I want to thank my husband for his encouragement and support of my ministry.

I'm so grateful to all those who read drafts of this book and provided their professional feedback (obviously any potential errors are mine): Dr. Sharon O'Brien of Catholics for Family Peace, Fr. Charles Dahm of the Domestic Violence Outreach program in the archdiocese of Chicago, and Dr. Christauria Welland of Pax in Familia, among so many others. Your love and support have given me the inspiration to keep moving forward.

A special note of gratitude goes out to Fr. Roch Drozdzik of St. Mary's Catholic Church in Goldsboro, NC, who generously allowed me to use his beautiful church as a setting for my author photos. A great pastor and an exceptional homilist, Fr. Roch has been a Spirit-filled blessing to the Catholic community of Goldsboro.

And, of course, I can't forget my siblings in Christ, those who have always had my back, supported my work, and encouraged my mission. I give immense thanks to Laura Ercolino and De Yarrison of Hope's Garden and You Are Made New Ministry, who helped me understand that I'm truly beloved by our divine Bridegroom. My heart is also with all my sister Roses at Hope's Garden, who have supported and encouraged me along the path toward healing and wholeness. Thanks also goes out to Fr. Benjamin Roberts of Our Lady of Lourdes Catholic Church in Monroe, NC—who helped me grow closer to St. Dymphna, the new patroness of domestic violence survivors—and to the spiritual family at my home parish of St. Brendan the Navigator in Camden, ME.

Table of Contents

Foreword

Domestic violence is rampant in the United States, and most people don't know it. Sadly, priests and pastoral ministers are also unaware. They don't realize a great number of their parishioners have suffered from domestic violence. According to the Centers for Disease Control and Prevention, at least one in four women has been either hit, sexually assaulted, or stalked by her spouse or partner. These victims, including some men, have been traumatized by it and would love to hear and see their church address the matter.

Jenny duBay has written a marvelous book, *Don't Plant Your Seeds Among the Thorns,* that covers the topic thoroughly and sensitively. As a survivor of domestic violence herself, she understands its deceitful trap, its traumatic impact as well as the courageous steps necessary to escape it. Significantly, her book addresses the problem from the point of view of the Christian faith. Jenny duBay plumbs the meaning of scripture and helps victims and survivors connect their faith with the evil they have experienced. She emphasizes the need for spiritual healing and guides the wounded along pathways to a new and regenerated life. Her book should be required reading for all parish ministers.

I have been a Catholic priest for 60 years, and for half of those years, I never spoke about domestic violence even though I saw some serious cases. Not until I hired a pastoral counselor on my parish staff did I learn how pervasive it is. The counselor told me one day that most of her clients were women, and most of them were victims of domestic violence. I had no idea, and I knew many of those women. But I didn't see the problem. She opened my eyes. She taught me how to discover the hurt and how to respond to it.

The more I learned about domestic violence, the more I talked about it. The more I talked about it, the more victims came to me for assistance. Our counselor was overwhelmed. In a few years, we had to hire five more counselors – three for victims, one for their children and another for those who cause harm. Victims came from far and wide because they received a faith-based response to their struggle. And this pastoral program brought life to our parish because many survivors wanted to give back to their community, volunteering in a wide variety of ministries.

Although the United States Bishops have written a beautiful pastoral letter about domestic violence, "When I Call for Help," few priests and pastoral ministers know about it, and fewer have read it. The bishops are clear and forceful. In the first paragraph, they state: "We declare as clearly and strongly as we can that violence against women, inside or outside the home, is *never* justified. Violence in any form is sinful; often, it is a crime as well." They conclude the letter stating, "We emphasize that no person is expected to stay in an abusive marriage."

Those are words of words of liberation for many women and some men. That is the position of the Catholic Church. We all have to get the message out.

Most people know someone affected by domestic violence, whether they grew up in a family plagued by it, experienced abuse in their own intimate relationship, or are currently struggling to free themselves from abuse. We all need to reach out to these victims or survivors and offer our compassionate understanding and support.

We have to help them understand they don't deserve abuse; they don't have to tolerate abuse, and they don't have to feel guilty about suffering abuse.

We thank Jenny duBay for helping get the word out about the Catholic Church's position. Her book adds greatly to the limited Catholic literature on the subject. She is also helping all of us, especially survivors, understand the multifaceted dynamics of domestic violence, the teaching of sacred scripture, and the ways to find safety, peace, and love.

Fr. Charles W. Dahm, O.P., Director
Archdiocese of Chicago Domestic Violence Outreach
www.domesticviolenceoutreach.org

Introduction

"A lover is simply the one who seeks what is profitable for the beloved: so that if any are not pursuing this, even if he makes ten thousand professions of his love, he is actually more hostile than any enemy."
(St. John Chrysostom, Commentary on 1 Corinthians 13)

The Catholic Church understands the true nature of marriage. The marital union isn't merely a piece of paper and a few words spoken between two people, followed by a fun party. It's not a gold band, or a promise to remain faithful—until disagreements pop up or someone more exciting comes along. For Catholics, marriage is a sacred sacrament, an indissoluble union that, according to *The Catechism of the Catholic Church,* is "a partnership of the whole of life … ordered toward the good of the spouses and the procreation and education of offspring" (CCC 1601). Love is "the fundamental and innate vocation of every human being" (CCC 1604).

Yet what happens when the indissoluble becomes desecrated, when the sacrament promised at the altar in the presence of God proves to have been a lie? What happens when the early excitement of a loving relationship and future family are replaced with anxiety, confusion, turmoil, and even cringing fear? Sacred Scripture describes well how such betrayal feels:

My heart is in anguish within me,
Fear and trembling come upon me,
and horror overwhelms me.

It is not an enemy who taunts me—
then I could bear it;
it is not an adversary who deals insolently with me—
then I could hide from him.
But it is you, my equal, my companion, my familiar friend.
We used to hold sweet converse together;
within God's house we walked in fellowship.
(Ps. 55:4,5,12-14)

Every day, around the world, millions of women are crushed by the trauma of living with a spouse who controls, mistreats or otherwise violates their sacred personhood. One out of every three women has been or currently is a victim of abuse within their own homes.[1] Yet even if you're among those statistics, you might be unaware of the truth of your situation. Instead, you may be full of self-blame and doubt—especially during the times when your spouse is acting kind, charming, even remorseful.

It's common for victims to minimize their experience, to believe their partner when he says they merely have "regular" relationship or communication problems. Victims often tell themselves, "It's really not that bad. Sure, sometimes he calls me stupid or an idiot, but at least he's never called me anything worse." Or, if he does make it a habit to hurl even the most brutal insults, a target may try to minimize the situation by thinking, "Well, at least he's never hit me." If

---

[1] World Health Organization, "Violence Against Women," https://www.who.int/news-room/fact-sheets/detail/violence-against-women

he is physically violent, "at least he's never broken a bone." If he has broken a bone, "At least I've never been knocked unconscious."

And on … and on.

This minimization isn't a deliberate effort to excuse the behavior of a partner who is acting abusively, but rather an unconscious defense mechanism that attempts to make sense of the nonsensical. To be the partner of an abusive spouse is to live in constant anxiety. Developing coping strategies is a necessary part of living in a toxic environment.

Yet living in that environment doesn't have to be permanent. Healing begins with awareness, education, support, and guidance from the Holy Spirit. These are all things this book will help you develop.

I know quite a bit about the emotional, psychological, and even physical trauma that comes as a result of domestic abuse, but I didn't arrive at this understanding on purpose. I didn't seek it out through in-depth research, courses, and professional certifications—all that came later. I learned about domestic abuse the painful way: hands-on. I've been in the middle of the fire and thankfully, through the grace of God, I've made it straight through.

That's why I'm here, now, in the vocation God has since blessed me with. Through suffering comes grace. That's what I aim to show you in this book: the ugly face of domestic abuse, and the glorious glow of healing.

But this book isn't about me—*Don't Plant Your Seeds Among Thorns* is also about you. If you've struggled in a chaotic, anxiety-filled, confusing, or violent relationship (keeping in mind that not all violence is physical) and are wondering if your spouse might be abusive, you've come to the right place. If you're utterly confused and need to find out what abuse actually is, you'll find out in the following pages. If you realize that you've been a victim and need help and healing, you'll find it here. If you're wondering how your sacramental marriage could have become so toxic, and what the Catholic Church teaches about abuse, divorce, and annulment, I provide information.

There have been countless secular books written on the topic of domestic violence, along with excellent podcasts, videos, articles, and other resources. However, there's a hole in the field of domestic violence awareness within the Catholic Church. Although domestic abuse can easily be considered a global epidemic, it's rarely talked about within local parish communities. Many—if not most—priests aren't trained to deal with a parishioner who may come to them with the confusion and anxiety that result from being abused by a spouse.

Fr. Chuck Dahm is the founder of the Domestic Violence Outreach program in the Archdiocese of Chicago, and I asked him what the educational requirements are for seminarians regarding domestic violence awareness. He confirmed that most seminaries in the U.S. don't offer courses on this crucial topic. In the United States Conference of Catholic Bishops (USCCB) document, "Catholic Response to Sexual and Domestic Violence and Abuse," the Church acknowledges that there's a tremendous lack of education among clergy and laity alike regarding intimate partner violence.

One area for growth is raising awareness … less than 1/3 of respondents reported priests or deacons preaching about sexual/domestic violence or abuse … Training is not often offered to marriage tribunal workers regarding domestic abuse ... The inclusion of information about sexual and domestic violence and abuse in marriage preparation was noted by just under half (45%) of respondents.[2]

This needs to change. And it is, but slowly.

In 1992 (revised in 2002) the USCCB issued a document entitled, "When I Call for Help: A Pastoral Response to Domestic Violence Against Women." In this publication, the U.S. bishops firmly state:

We emphasize that no person is expected to stay in an abusive marriage. Some abused women believe that church teaching on the permanence of marriage requires them to stay in an abusive relationship ... Violence and abuse, not divorce, break up a marriage.[3]

Well-established organizations such as Catholics for Family Peace (http://www.catholicsforfamilypeace.org), Pax in Familia (http://paxinfamilia.org), and the Domestic Violence Outreach program through the Archdiocese of Chicago (https://pvm.arch-chicago.org/human-dignity-solidarity/domestic-violence-outreach)

---

[2] United States Conference of Catholic Bishops, "Catholic Response to Sexual and Domestic Violence and Abuse," https://www.usccb.org/issues-and-action/marriage-and-family/marriage/domestic-violence/upload/Catholic-Response-to-Sexual-and-Domestic-Violence-Report-Final.pdf

[3] United States Conference of Catholic Bishops, "When I Call for Help: A Pastoral Response to Domestic Violence Against Women," https://www.usccb.org/topics/marriage-and-family-life-ministries/when-i-call-help-pastoral-response-domestic-violence

are doing excellent work educating church leaders and domestic abuse advocates within various dioceses across the United States. Even so, up until now a book for abuse survivors, written from a Catholic perspective and detailing what abuse is, what can be done, and the support available to Catholics in sacramental marriages, has been lacking.

I aim to fill that void.

Targets of intimate partner violence aren't stuck or doomed to a life of confusion, neglect, mistreatment, crazy-making, gaslighting, circular communication, name-calling, criticism, and all the rest. "Wives must be submissive to their husbands" (Eph 5:22) has long been taken out of context. This verse is also a victim of abuse—but more on that in chapter six.

In this book, I cover such topics as what domestic abuse is, the trauma of sexual assault and coercion, verbal attacks and isolation, and the evils of manipulative control within intimate relationships. I also discuss the sacrament of marriage, what *indissoluble* means, betrayal of the marital bond, and the Catholic declaration of nullity (more commonly known as an annulment). Biblical misconceptions and how to heal are also discussed.

But, unlike most books on domestic violence, I also examine the possibility that an abusive partner might change. I do this for several reasons. First, this is a question countless women have asked me. They want to know if there's any hope that the gentle and seemingly kind man they fell in love with can permanently return, or if he never truly existed. Unfortunately, there's no black-and-white answer to that question. It's true that throughout this book I'll talk about the possibility of changing, and my outlook tends to be more optimistic than you might expect. If you've read anything else about domestic violence, particularly information that discusses the "narcissistic abuser," my positive outlook on the possibility of change may seem at odds with what nearly everyone else is saying.

And it is. The vast majority of publications aren't hopeful about change, and some even label all abusive personalities as selfish people devoid of empathy and with no desire whatsoever to live their lives in a new and loving way.

Sadly, that's often true—except when it's not.

We're all made in the image and likeness of God (Gen 1:26), and—in the words of the Vatican II document, *Gaudium et Spes*— we all "bear within ourselves an eternal seed."[4] Whether or not we allow that seed to blossom is another matter. It's important not to categorize all abusive personalities as if they're exactly the same, because that's simply not true. In chapter nine, I detail the four classic "abuser types," how they differ, and what it takes to authentically change.

Regardless of which of the four categories an abusive person more closely resembles, it's crucial to remember that we must always err on the side of caution. If a situation isn't physically safe, hope of reconciliation is never recommended. In that case, a solid safety plan designed with the help of professionals is essential since the most severe violence (including murder) happens when a woman is leaving or has already left her partner. Appendix D will provide resources for creating a solid safety plan. This is crucial, particularly if your partner:

---

[4]*Gaudium et Spes,*18, in *The Sixteen Documents of Vatican II*, ed. Marianne Lorraine Trouvé (Boston: Pauline Books & Media, 1999).

- Has already been physically abusive
- Owns a weapon or weapons
- Threatens violence
- Threatens to kill his spouse, children, pets, or himself
- Goes on drinking binges
- Is involved with drugs
- Victim feels constant terror, fear and anxiety, even if she can't pinpoint why

If you've been a target of abuse, you need to heal, and that's the aim of this book: education, which will then lead to healthy empowerment of your true self. An honest assessment of your personal situation is crucial. All this, and more and will be covered in greater detail in the chapters to come.

At the back of the book, you'll find an appendix containing several sections, including a series of questions to determine if your relationship may be abusive, a full list of resources, how to craft a safety plan, and more. I also include a list of abuse terms, which provides an easy reference to common phrases and words used in this book to describe various tactics of manipulation.

In closing, I need to mention a few housekeeping items. First, throughout the following pages I'll be referring to the individual who uses abusive tactics in the relationship as "he" and the target victim as "she." I realize men are also victims of abuse. However, the vast majority of domestic violence victims are women—statistically, in 85% of cases.[5] If you happen to be a male target of abuse, please feel free to change the pronouns around in your head to make a more enjoyable reading experience. Really, I won't be offended.

Another thing we should always remember is that we're all survivors, which is a healthier viewpoint than thinking of ourselves as victims. It's certainly true that we're victims as well—victims not only of intimate partner violence but of betrayal of the worst kind, of heartbreak and a complete shattering of all we thought to be true about our spouse and our sacred marriage. However, we can't allow ourselves to be victims of despondency and despair, which is what will happen if we focus on a victimhood status.

We're survivors. Whether you're now free of your confusing and destructive relationship or still involved with your partner, if you're reading this book, *you are a survivor.* And you don't have to travel this path alone. All of us who have endured the immense suffering of domestic abuse are more resilient than we realize. All of us are still here and will be stronger for our experience.

However, for the sake of clarity I use *victim, survivor,* and *target* interchangeably—but always remember, above all you're a survivor.

I also want to mention that I have a degree in theology, not psychology (although I am a certified trauma-informed Catholic life coach). As I mentioned in the beginning of this introduction, my

---

[5] Domesticshelters.org, "Domestic Violence Statistics: The Hard Truth About Domestic Violence," https://www.domesticshelters.org/articles/statistics/domestic-violence-statistics. See also John Gottman, Ph.D. and Neil Jacobson, Ph.D., *When Men Batter Women: New Insights into Ending Abusive Relationships* (NY, NY: Simon & Schuster, 1998), 34-36 and Christauria Welland, Psy.D., "Violence and Abuse in Catholic & Christian Families: Preparing an Effective and Compassionate Pastoral Response."

experience in domestic abuse is because I've "been there, done that," and as a result I've now dedicated my life to research, education, and helping others heal.

I'm the founder of Create Soul Space, a Catholic ministry that supports, empowers, and encourages domestic abuse survivors. I'm also an ICF-accredited trauma-informed life coach specializing in helping women heal and recover their true, God-given selves after the trauma they've endured. In addition, I author two active blogs:

- https://www.createsoulspace.org
- https://www.prodigalparishioner.com

am a freelance writer for numerous Catholic publications, and serve as a facilitator at Hope's Garden.

- https://hopesgarden.com/join-our-community/

And now, this book.

Always remember that no matter how dark your day may seem, how crazy and confusing your life, how much you feel unloved and rejected, "No one after lighting a lamp puts it in a cellar or under a bed, but puts it on a stand, that those who enter may see the light" (Luke 8:16; 11:33). You have that light. You are that light. You can let your Christ-light shine again, no matter how dim it may now seem. There is hope. Christ is your hope. God doesn't want you to plant your seeds among thorns (Jer. 4:3).

Chapter One

An Overview of Domestic Abuse

"The blow of a whip raises a welt,
but a blow of the tongue crushes the bones."

(Sirach 28:17)

When the topic domestic violence is mentioned, people often visualize black eyes, broken bones, and clenched fists. However, manipulation and control over another individual takes many forms. Domestic abuse can violate a person not only physically but emotionally, spiritually, psychologically, sexually, and financially.

Bruises, broken bones, and smashed faces shout obvious violence, traumatic for the victim and outwardly visible. A broken spirit isn't as visible, and bruises to the soul are easily buried with a false smile and cover-up stories to hide the truth. Yet in a multitude of studies and interviews, survivors have consistently affirmed that emotional, psychological, and verbal abuse are even more traumatic than broken bones. All forms of abuse leave scars and bruises in the soul.

These destructive actions aren't isolated events. Everyone makes mistakes, saying and doing things they later come to regret. They soon recognize their slip-ups, make genuine reparation, and don't repeat the toxic behavior. An abusive relationship, on other hand, is a pattern of attitudes and actions that create a confusing, terrifying, fragile, and crazy-making atmosphere within what should be the sacred space of the home. The abuse is repeated, again and again. Even if months go by with no obvious incident, eventually the same pattern reappears—and, as the years go by, the pattern reappears with increasing frequency. Some examples of domestic abuse include:

- name-calling and insults
- spousal neglect
- extreme and controlling jealousy
- constant criticism, both overt and covert
- threats to kill or harm one's partner, children, pets, or self
- destruction of property
- forced vaccination, sterilization, or abortion
- sexual assault or coercion
- blaming others or constantly making excuses for negative behaviors
- physical violence
- undermining and belittling
- being deliberately evasive in conversation, omitting information, and other forms of lying
- circular talk (conversations become dizzying and impossible to follow)
- the victim isn't allowed to have opinions separate from her partner
- intimidation by subtle threats, looks, actions, or tone of voice

The consistent, continual pattern of domestic abuse is dizzying and bewildering, especially since an individual with abusive traits quite often displays shows a "Dr. Jekyll and Mr. Hyde" personality. He can often be charming and sweet, and during those times the victim will feel overwhelming relief and gratitude. Eventually, though, he becomes "Mr. Hyde" again, exploding in aggressive rage or covert criticism, often employing manipulative tactics that are more dangerous because of their subtly.

These tactics are all part of the abuse cycle.

The Abuse Cycle

Bait / adoration. The abuse cycle is the recurring pattern that keeps playing out, again and again, in most toxic relationships. First there's the "adoration" stage, in which your spouse is contrite, kind, seemingly empathetic and loving. I refer to this as the first phase of the cycle because the grooming, "love bombing" aspect of a relationship is what a target first sees during the initial dating period, before the abuse cycle begins to revolve in earnest. This stage feels wonderful and is an enormous relief after a cycle of mistreatment.

It's at this point that you begin to feel change is truly possible. It's this promise, this hope, that keeps most victims from leaving. What if there's a chance he'll become the caring man you once thought he was? Marriage is a sacred vow. It can't be dumped if there's hope, can it? Yet when the cycle repeats over and over, through the years, hope begins to deteriorate.

In reality, this isn't the stage of a relationship where authentic love or repentance occurs. It's actually the "bait" phase of the cycle, where you're pulled back into a romantic connection with promises of change, expressions of undying love, and the relief of what seems to be much-needed respect and empathy. This is a grooming technique that abusive personalities use to regain control of the relationship. However, it doesn't indicate true remorse—just like the peanut butter in a mouse trap doesn't indicate a true meal.

Calm. Eventually—in a matter of days, weeks, sometimes even months—the adoration and love start to fade. The relationship enters a period of calm, where abuse is either so covert it's barely detected, or continues to be absent. Your partner may no longer be giving you roses and making grand professions of love, but at least you're still experiencing respite from his mistreatment. There are promises of protection and security, even if unspoken.

You may still hear a few apologies in this stage of the cycle, but again it's crucial to be vigilant and alert. Any apology that has a "but" in it isn't authentic ("I'm sorry I called you stupid, but I was drunk," "I'm sorry I smashed your vase, but you triggered me"). In the "calm" phase of the abuse cycle you may feel you can breathe again, and perhaps even trust again. In this stage your partner may ignore his abuse altogether, as if he never did anything wrong—a tactic of denial that makes you feel as if you exaggerated things and that your relationship is fine.

It's during the "calm" stage that your self-doubt begins to deepen as you further question your perceptions, your memory, and your intuition.

Tension building. All too soon, the "tension building" stage of the abuse cycle begins. You can feel something simmering, even though it may not be overtly obvious. Your partner may turn cold or critical, silent, and brooding, or he may constantly harass you with a barrage of little things that soon become overwhelming. Often the shift is so subtle that it's hard to explain in words, yet it can certainly be felt.

Abusive Incident. Next comes the "rage stage"—the explosion, the outburst, the full-fledged Mr. Hyde coming out like a roaring lion, waiting for someone (you) to devour (1 Peter 5:8). If someone who's acting abusively is particularly covert, this stage may not take the form of violent outbursts such as punching walls, vicious shouting, and fierce anger. Instead, it may manifest in subtle accusations, heartbreaking name-calling, various levels of betrayal, increased gaslighting, and more. You might experience all the above, or a mixture of tactics. Aggressors are predictable in their unpredictability.

The wheel has made a full rotation. You're back to where you were before. Your spouse is apologetic, hearts and red roses appear, you begin to feel hopeful yet again …

Trauma Bonding

Abusive incidents are traumatic, confusing, heartbreaking and devastating—but even more so because they're alternated with good times. These good times foster feelings of increased love, devotion, and gratitude. As an emotionally (and perhaps physically) battered woman who is psychologically tortured by your husband's manipulative tactics, you likely feel immense gratitude when the relationship suddenly becomes "normal" again.

Because of the "bait/adoration" stage of the abuse cycle, you've likely formed a trauma bond to your partner. This type of connection isn't authentic love, but it certainly feels like it.

Rather than the abuse causing you to want to run—and run fast—to get away from the toxic environment you're in, the return of kind, loving treatment and goodwill leaves you craving more. Not more abuse, of course, but more love. Additionally, the good times foster hope that perhaps he'll finally change.

The intermittent state of misplaced hope will keep you hooked not just emotionally, but hormonally as well, saturating your brain with an overwhelming chemical cocktail. This cocktail consists of oxytocin (the "feel good/attachment" hormone), cortisol, adrenaline, norepinephrine (hormones that "work together to consolidate and reconsolidate fear-based memories"), and serotonin.[6]

Paradoxically, this causes you to become more attached to your abuser. The unpredictability of the times of love, caring and affection becomes a powerful form of addiction. When good times are sporadic, interwoven with acts of abuse and mistreatment, the reward circuits in the brain are intensified. This is also why you tend to have intense loving feelings toward the Dr. Jekyll side of your partner, constantly viewing him on an empathetic level even when the abuse escalates.

---

[6] Shahida Arabi, *Power: Surviving & Thriving After Narcissistic Abuse* (Brooklyn, NY: Thought Catalog Books, 2017), 217-220. See also Patrick J. Carnes, Ph.D. with Bonnie Phillips, Ph.D., *The Betrayal Bond: Breaking Free of Exploitive Relationship* (Deerfield Beach, FL: Health Communications, Inc., 2019), 38.

The irony is that those who are trauma bonded become attached to the very person who happens to be the cause of their anguish. You're in a state of shock and distress and turn to the source of the distress for relief from the crushing fear, anxiety, and bewilderment. It's like living in an upside-down world, where the truth is revealed to be a delusion and safety is impossible because the one who is supposed to keep you safe is the same person holding you prisoner.

Characteristics and Traits of People Who Act Abusively Toward Others

Individuals who use abuse to control their relationships come from all walks of life, every ethnicity, and can be found around the globe in alarmingly large numbers. However, despite the diversity of each person there are features that are common to most aggressors. Not all abusive individuals carry all these characteristics, but if you recognize your spouse in a couple of these, consider that your marriage may be unhealthy. If several of these descriptions sound familiar, chances are high that you're in a toxic relationship.

It's also crucial to remember that individuals abuse on a spectrum—all situations and relationships are different, even though the characteristics, traits, manipulative tactics, and motivations are eerily similar. Some aggressive people display more traits, others less, although abuse does tend to escalate as the years go on—unless a person has the courage to seek help, to fully admit what he has done, and to pursue authentic change.

But I'll talk more about that later. For now, here's a list of some of the typical characteristics of abusive personalities.

Lack of core identity. Most individuals with abusive personalities seek control, manipulation, belittling, one-upmanship and the need to always be right because they lack an inner sense of self. They're often not in touch with the truth of their God-given identity but instead feel an emptiness where self ought to be. Full of a deep sense of toxic shame, these individuals hide from themselves by trying to control others.

Excessive jealousy and possessiveness. Another nearly universal trait is extreme, overbearing, unwarranted and highly-controlling jealousy. This extreme possessiveness is irrational, and greatly affects the target's social life and ability to feel comfortable in social situations. Lenore E. Walker, a pioneer in the field of domestic violence awareness, has noted that "anyone who is kind to the battered woman becomes a target of the batterer's sexual jealousy. This includes her male co-workers, next-door neighbor, supermarket clerk, bartender … and so on."[7]

Your partner will likely mask his controlling jealousy under several pretenses, such as claiming to be insecure about his past or blaming you for dressing flirtatiously. He may also claim that he's merely trying to protect you from "male predators" or that he suspects you're unfaithful or thinking about being unfaithful. He may also say that he's jealous only because of how madly, deeply in love with you he is. The USCCB acknowledges, "While there is no one

---

[7] Lenore E. Walker, *The Battered Woman* (NY, NY: William Morrow, An Imprint of HarperCollins, 1979), 114.

type, men who abuse share some common characteristics. They tend to be extremely jealous, possessive, and easily angered."[8]

All the excuses your spouse may have for his jealousness are just that—excuses, an attempt to minimize and even normalize his behavior, a way to brainwash you into feeling sorry for him or accepting the blame.

Domestic violence expert Lundy Bancroft, author of the best-selling book *Why Does He Do That? Inside the Minds of Angry and Controlling Men,* has worked extensively with both victims and perpetrators for decades. He confirms his observation of jealous behavior among abusive men:

> The jealous guy is sure to have excuses—that he's this way because his last partner cheated on him, or because his mother cheated on his father, or because he's never had such a beautiful partner and he's afraid you'll leave him. And that's what they are: excuses.[9]

Jealousy isn't always limited to accusations of flirting and other forms of infidelity; a person with abusive tendencies can be jealous of your successes, your children, and your relationships with anyone other than him. All this eventually leads to self-isolation. It gets to be too much to deal with his rages after a fun, innocent girls' night

---

[8] USCCB, "When I Call for Help."

[9] Lundy Bancroft and Jac Patrissi, *Should I Stay or Should I Go? A Guide to Knowing if Your Relationship Can—and Should—Be Saved* (NY, NY: Berkley Books, 2001), 359.

out, or the barrage of questions after returning home from the gym. It's easier—and feels safer—to simply stay at home.

If you find yourself altering your innocent and healthy social life because of your spouse's attitudes, that's a sure sign of domestic abuse.

Yet there's a flipside to extreme jealousy. A small subset of people with abusive traits—generally those of a grandiose rather than covert nature—not only don't mind other men gawking at "their" woman, but actually encourage it. They urge (or force) her to dress in sexy ways, then parade her around as if she's one of their flashy possessions. "Look at my expensive Porsche! Look at my gorgeous girlfriend!" They enjoy how the attention reflects on them.

Even though outwardly this is the opposite of the jealous type, the motivation behind the action is the same—possessiveness.

St. Paul, in writing to the Galatians, makes a list of the works of flesh versus the fruits of the Spirit—two very different lists, "in fact, they are opposed to each other" (Gal 5:17). Among the works of the flesh, which are "against the Spirit" (5:17), St. Paul includes jealousy, along with "enmity, strife … anger, selfishness, dissension, party spirit, envy, drunkenness …" (5:20). The fruits of the Spirit include the opposite of jealousy—love, as well as "joy, peace, patience, kindness, goodness, faithfulness, gentleness, self-control" (5:22). Those who indulge in the works of the flesh and are possessively jealous create dissension and "shall not inherit the kingdom of God" (5:21).

That's a terrifying thought, and a dire warning.

Full of rage*.* Whether simmering beneath the surface yet covertly masked behind a wall of silence or overtly expressed in violent fits of accusation and name-calling, those who use abuse to manipulate relationships tend to be filled with contempt, resentment, and rage. When that rage explodes and your Dr. Jekyll turns into Mr. Hyde yet again, extreme anxiety, panic, confusion, or despondency usually result. As the abuse cycle continues, the psychological and emotional damage can be profound, even paralyzing.

Hypocritical. An abuser forces his victim to follow a separate set of rules than he does. It's fine for him to flirt with other women, watch pornography, or commit some other act of infidelity, but if you so much as ask the produce guy at your local supermarket if the broccoli is fresh, your spouse will fly into a frothing rage and accuse you of having an affair. (With the broccoli or with the produce guy? The resulting circular talk is so confusing it can be difficult to tell.)

He can go out to bars as often as he wants, but if you go out for coffee with a friend, you'll get grilled with so many accusatory questions that your head will start to spin as heartbroken frustration grips your spine in a tight mass of stress. He can have his own opinions, but if yours don't precisely match his, he'll accuse you of disrespecting him or even hating him.

The examples of hypocrisy are long and varied, but you get the idea: "Do what I say, but you're not allowed to do what I do."

Jesus was blunt about such personalities: "Woe to you, hypocrites! For you are like whitewashed tombs, which outwardly appear beautiful, but within they are full of dead men's bones and all uncleanness" (Matt. 23:27).

Masters at projection. If he falsely accuses you of something, you can be fairly certain it's the exact act, thought, or emotion he's doing, thinking, or feeling. This is what projection is all about—attributing his own actions and motivations onto you.

Projection is actually a fairly good way of figuring out what he's up to. For example, if he accuses you of being unfaithful, be on your guard for any unfaithful behavior on his part. And remember, infidelity isn't limited to the extreme of having sex with another person—unfaithfulness in marriage covers a wide range of behaviors, from pornography use, masturbation, flirting with women, or even having sexual/adulterous thoughts.

Often an abuser will unconsciously project his own tactics onto you, his victim. He'll complain that you're controlling, inconsiderate, disrespectful, untrustworthy, selfish, rude, unfeeling, hopeless, impossible, mean, critical, manipulative, unloving and more. He may even claim that you're the abusive one—that's a very common accusation for an aggressor to make, one that's to be expected in toxic relationships.

Chronic lying. People who act abusively are, almost without exception, excellent liars. Lying has become a well-practiced art, and one he's so skilled at that he's reached the level of near-perfection. He can look people directly in the eye and, with a straight and even empathetic-seeming expression, tell complete falsehoods without compunction. Because of his skill in lying, most victims are completely unaware of the deception that's being thrown at them.

And, as scary and psychologically off-balance as this sounds, he's likely so skilled at lying that quite often he fools himself, honestly believing his own twisted version of things. This high level of delusion is the result of unconscious defense mechanisms combined with cognitive distortions, which severs reality in order to allow the fragile inner self to make excuses and blame others for his behavior. It also feeds his need to play the victim rather than the perpetrator.[10]

Those who use abuse to control their relationships initially present themselves as dependable, honest, trustworthy, safe and ideal. Their spouses are convinced they have open communication and can talk about anything—until something happens, small or large, sudden or accumulated, that makes them realize that lying has been a part of their supposedly-sacred marriage from the very beginning.

This becomes all the more confusing because lying doesn't consist merely of telling outright untruths but also acts of omission, deliberate vagueness, and half-truths.

The Catechism of the Catholic Church is quite firm about the sin of dishonesty:

> By its very nature, lying is to be condemned … The deliberate intention of leading a neighbor into error by saying things contrary to the truth constitutes a failure in justice and charity … Since it violates the virtue of truthfulness, a lie does real violence to another. It contains the seed of discord and all consequent evils. Lying is destructive to society; it undermines trust … it tears apart the fabric of social relationships (CCC 2485, 2486).

---

[10] Erin Leonard, Ph.D., "Does a Narcissist Believe His or Her Own Lies?" Psychology Today, https://www.psychologytoday.com/us/blog/peaceful-parenting/201906/does-narcissist-believe-his-or-her-own-lies

The gravest lie is betrayal of the marriage vow, the promise to "be true to you … to love and honor you all the days of my life." Lying and abuse are the opposite of loving, honoring, and being true.

Sacred Scripture is clear on this topic. The wisdom of Proverbs states, "lying lips are an abomination to the LORD" (12:22), while the book of Revelation goes so far as to group liars with murderers. "But as for the cowardly, the faithless, the polluted, as for murderers, fornicators, sorcerers, idolaters, and all liars, their lot shall be in the lake that burns with fire and brimstone, which is the second death" (21:8).

Ouch.

Misattributions. People with abusive personalities tend to assume the worst in their partners, viewing them as an adversary rather than a lover and equal partner. Someone with this mindset seems to believe that all your motives, actions and decisions have negative intentions, or that you're deliberately trying to hurt him.

Researchers Amy Holzworth-Munroe and Glenn Hutchinson studied *misattributions*—flawed beliefs about someone else's behavior—and found that abusive men were

> much more likely to attribute the most negative intentions to their wives' behavior. These men were much more likely to be convinced that she was *trying* to make him angry, hurt his feelings, put him down get something for herself, or pick a fight. The researchers also found that when the men

perceived a situation of abandonment or rejection, they were particularly likely to respond with bad behavior.[11]

Self-orientated. Individuals prone to abuse display a high level of narcissistic traits. This is particularly difficult to detect in someone with a fragile, covertly manipulative personality, yet it's always there. Although a covert/fragile attention seeker is trickier to spot than someone who acts grandiose and overtly demands to be the center of attention, he's no less insistent that everything be about him. His demands are all-consuming, and they always have to be on his terms—when he wants, how he wants it.

In conversations, the attention seeker tends to talk *at* people, rather than *to* them—and he doesn't take the hint when others try to make non-verbal gestures of boredom or frustration. Should the focus of a conversation stray to someone or something other than him, he'll twist the topic back to make himself the center once again.

Expectations of mind reading. An individual with an abusive mindset assumes his victim can read his thoughts, and his unspoken demands must be immediately catered to. Your spouse may expect you to act or react in a certain way, speak exactly as he requires, and give him the attention, emotion, or action that he wants—all without him having to ask. You're supposed to know what he wants and when he wants it (apparently, he's forgotten that crystal balls and psychic mind-reading are forbidden by the Church). This, to him, isn't an

---

[11] David B. Wexler, Ph.D., *When Good Men Behave Badly* (Oakland, CA: New Harbinger Publications, Inc., 2004), 9.

unrealistic expectation, impossible to fulfill, but rather a matter of "respect," and there's hell to pay if you don't comply. As former domestic abuser Austin James admits:

> I very rarely verbalized my expectations to anyone, yet at the same time I kept a very detailed score as to whether those expectations were being met or not. I carefully monitored other people and situations and could easily get upset whenever I didn't see the outcome that I was looking for ... It was a never-ending cycle for me: 1) have expectations, 2) don't verbalize those expectations, and 3) be upset when those expectations were not met. Expectations trapped me in an almost daily pattern of getting angry about something or someone.[12]

Conversely, the abuser will assume he can read *your* mind. If you're having a bad day for any reason whatsoever, he'll feel it's his right to jump into your head and assume your low mood is all about him. He'll ascribe negative motives and thoughts to your most innocent and well-meaning comments or actions. He'll tell you what you're thinking and what you believe, and he's nearly always way off-base—yet you can't convince him of that. As always, he's right and you're wrong—even when it comes to your own mind.

---

[12] Austin James, *Emotional Abuse, Silent Killer of Marriage: A 30-Year Abuser Speaks Out* (self-published, 2016), 22 and 23.

Blame shifters. It's not his fault—regardless of what "it" is. The bad things that happen to him or in your relationship are nearly always blamed on you. When called out on his abusive behavior, he blames his childhood, his ex, his job, stress, alcohol, co-workers, or "you made me do it."

However, *there is no excuse for abuse.* No matter how damaging someone's childhood may have been, how much stress they're experiencing at work, or any other external circumstance, that's not an excuse for mistreating another human being, nor is it an excuse for blaming others for the consequences of one's own choices and actions.

We're all graced with free will. If we misuse that God-given gift, the results are our responsibility, not another's.

Isolators. If your spouse displays signs of excessive jealousy, he likely doesn't want you to develop or maintain outside friendships, nor will he permit you to hear opinions that vary from his own. If you have outside friendships, you might get clued in to the fact that there's more out there. You might begin to realize that there's something severely wrong with your own relationship, an awareness an abuser wants to avoid at all costs (whether consciously or not).

This is such an important and foundational topic that I've dedicated chapter four solely to the tactic of isolation.

Other characteristics of an abusive personality include:

- Demeaning

- Disrespectful and disparaging toward previous partners, parents, or other people who are or were close to him
- Disrespectful toward you
- Highly contemptuous
- Unwilling to acknowledge reality or twists the truth and believes his own version of events, often protecting his beliefs with extreme defensiveness
- Prone to splitting (black and white thinking—you're either all good or all bad, with no in-between)
- Is highly critical
- Lacks true empathy, even if he may do a good job of appearing empathetic
- Uses intimidation as a tool for control
- Pressures you for intimacy and makes life very awkward or uncomfortable if you refuse
- Insists on making decisions for you
- Destroys your property
- Threatens to hurt himself if you leave
- Threatens to gain full custody of the children if you leave
- Embarrasses you in front of others
- Tells you you're nothing without him or will never be able to find another partner as good as him

These are only a few examples, but enough for you to get a good idea of what to look out for in your relationship. Again, most people who act abusively toward others won't display all these traits and there has to be a consistent repetition of behaviors, not merely an isolated mistake. Abuse is a cycle and a pattern.

Always remember 1 Peter 5:8: Be alert, be vigilant, be on your guard. Abusive tactics are evil assaults that are inherently destructive, particularly when they're subtle and shrouded in a false persona of caring. Although there may never be bruises on the body, abuse of any kind creates bruises to the spirit that are deep, shattering, and can be ultimately life-threatening unless thoroughly healed.

Intimate partner violence is a scourge, an epidemic, and a horrific environment for anyone to have to endure. That's why you don't have to endure it. There is hope, and help. There is redemption and healing in your future, if you let it enter. "For I know the plans I have for you, says the LORD, plans for welfare and not for evil, to give you a future and a hope" (Jer. 29:11).

If you're still not certain whether or not your relationship is abusive, you may want to take the quiz in Appendix B.

Chapter Two

The Serpent and the Maiden:
The Dangers of Covert Abuse

"At the root of every act of violence against one's neighbor there is a concession to the 'thinking' of the evil one, the one who 'was a murderer from the beginning' (John 8:44)."
(St. John Paul II, *The Gospel of Life*)

The title of this chapter sounds like an exciting fairy tale, but abusive relationships don't fall into the "happily ever after" category. Controlling, manipulative and abusive marriages are more like a Grimm's fairy tale than a classic Disney movie.

Most confusing of all is a partner who acts abusively in a covert way, such as using subtle control tactics under the guise of "love," "protection," and "caring." These are the individuals who manipulate with a hidden agenda, trying to compensate for their low self-esteem and feelings of shame by gaining power over others in hidden and subtle ways. It can be tricky to detect their motives, especially if they're not even admitting to themselves that they're inflicting a high level of traumatic abuse on their loved ones.

Don't Let the Tricksters Trick You

One of my clients (I'll call her "Juliet") has given me permission to share her story. She told me that when she and her husband were newly married and she was still in the haze of not understanding what was wrong with her relationship, they went out for dinner. After paying the check and getting ready to leave, a strange and perhaps prophetic thing happened in the lobby of the restaurant, something that has stuck with her ever since.

An elderly gentleman was standing at the exit as Juliet approached to leave the restaurant, his back to her and her husband, silently gazing out of the doorway as he waited for his ride to pull up. Without warning he spun around and stared at Juliet, unblinking and unapologetic, as if to give her an urgent message.

"Don't let the tricksters trick you, because if you turn around they'll get you in the end," he said, then just as abruptly he turned back around and walked out the door.

Was he aware of something Juliet was failing to see? Was he trying to give her a warning?

Of course, she'll never know the motive behind the man's sudden and seemingly inexplicable message. Had it been given to him by the Holy Spirit, a direct warning to help her be on her guard, or was it the senile ramblings of an elderly person? Juliet doesn't believe the man was senile, and his words struck her so thoroughly that they were instantly seared into her memory, verbatim, and have refused to let go ever since. She's told me that it certainly feels like a purposeful and God-given message, something that has kept bursting into her mind, again and again, as she's repeatedly traveled through the cycle of abuse over the course of too many years. In fact, well over a decade later, the message feels stronger to Juliet than ever before.

Don't let the tricksters trick you, because if you turn around they'll get you in the end …

That's what covert abuse attempts to do.

Unbalanced Egoism

People with manipulative personalities tend to be extremely self-focused—in other words, narcissistic. Many people assume that individuals with high levels of narcissistic traits are easy to spot because they're pompous and love to tell everyone how great they are. However, those characteristics describe only one type of narcissism, that of a "grandiose narcissist." To be subtly narcissistic is less easy to detect, unless you happen to be an intimate partner forced to endure the consequences of unbalanced, abusive qualities in your spouse.

When toxic behavior is covert, it's easy to be so trusting that you can be tricked by your supposedly-loving spouse. Covert narcissism is also called *vulnerable narcissism* or *fragile narcissism* because that's just what the individual with this trait is. His sense of self is flimsy, which puts him on the defensive. He believes he's worthless but barely admits his profound sense of shame even to himself, instead burying it through escape techniques such a drugs and alcohol, or through a "counterattack." Rather than facing his problems head-on, he ignores them by blaming others, turning to criticism and projection to hide his own shame, and making his spouse feel as if she's the one who's defective and wrong. He's convinced that the cause of all his life's issues reside in things external to himself rather than his behaviors. And, he truly believes his twisted version of reality.

When someone has an unbalanced level of egoistic traits, they tend to be controlling, overly jealous, in need of admiration and constant reassurance of their value, low or completely lacking in empathy, full of anger with an underlying and bottomless sense of shame, hypersensitive to criticism, and prone to blaming others for their issues. If you've noticed that I've just repeated the same character traits as I described in chapter one ("An Overview of Domestic Abuse"), then you get the idea.

Gaslighting

One of the primary tactics of emotional abusers is gaslighting. Entire articles have been written on the topic of gaslighting, but, in short, it's a type of psychological manipulation that causes you to question your own reality, thoughts, intuition, beliefs, and opinions. Common side-effects of chronic gaslighting include depression and a foreboding sense of hopelessness. Joy has been replaced with confusion and insecurity. You've forgotten yourself, your own personal Eden.

Examples of gaslighting include diverting a conversation, claiming to have forgotten discussions or situations, outright denial, trivializing, withholding, and countering. Basically, gaslighting is any tactic that attempts to make you feel as if your memory is faulty, your reality is unreal, and your sanity is questionable. You're often told you're too naïve, not smart enough to know better/not as smart as him, can't be relied upon to remember properly/has a worse memory than him, or any other myriad of excuses employed by manipulators to attain their end goal of control.

Abuse is evil—the Most Reverend Ricardo Ramírez even calls it a "virulent evil."[13] This isn't to say that those who employ abusive techniques to manipulate and control others are inherently evil people, rather that the actions themselves are evil. This may be a particularly confusing truth to come to terms with, because during the "love bombing" or "bait/adoration" stage of the abuse cycle, your husband again acts like the man you fell in love with—kind, caring, loving and genuine, a great father and the perfect spouse. He may also play the victim, which creates a high level of empathy and support towards him (a technique that further solidifies the trauma bond).

This sort of psychological manipulation causes a bewildering sense of cognitive dissonance. With two conflicting ideas swirling around your head at the same time, it's inevitable that you'll experience great distress and confusion—for example, arriving at the realization that there's an abusive pattern to your marriage, yet still holding hope that this most recent "love bombing" stage will be permanent and that your husband will suddenly be kind and caring all the time, not merely in fits and starts. It's heartbreaking to finally have to come to the terms with the fact that this "love bombing" stage is part of the cycle of manipulation and isn't reality—and, as the relationship progresses, the "calm" and "bait/adoration" stages

---

[13] Most Reverend Ricardo Ramírez, C.S.B., "Speaking the Unspeakable: A Pastoral Letter on Domestic Violence," accessed through the online course "Violence and Abuse in Catholic & Christian Families: Preparing an Effective and Compassionate Pastoral Response," Pax in Familia, https://health-transformations.learnworlds.com/course/violence-and-abuse-in-catholic-and-christian-families

of the cycle tend to grow shorter and shorter, sometimes disappearing altogether.

We would be doing ourselves a disservice if we ignored the facts. Abuse is contrary to life, love, and goodness. To make this bold claim, we need to go back to the story of world's first abuser, a creature who used gaslighting to manipulate his victim. This "first abuser" was none other than that evil serpent who appeared at the beginning of Sacred Scripture and who, at the very end of the Bible, was revealed to be Satan (Gen 3:1 and Rev 12:9). The literary devices used in the first chapters of Genesis hold potent meaning and can teach us numerous lessons.

In Genesis 3, we read about the serpent's trickster ploy to manipulate Eve into committing the first sin, eating the fruit of the tree of the knowledge of good and evil. "Now the serpent was more subtle than any other wild creature that the LORD God had made" (Gen 3:1). He was sly, a trickster. The most damaging type of manipulator—cunning and covert. Whether consciously or not, those who manipulate their relationships through abusive tactics are exploiters of the kindness, empathy, and any potential vulnerability of their targets. In other words, they're bullies of the cruelest sort.

The story about the serpent's tactics against Eve were more than a mere trick. They were covert gaslighting, twisting Eve's perceptions and her understanding of God's reality, convincing her that he was the "good guy," the one with her best interests at heart, while God wasn't to be trusted. This represents pure projection, another common tactic of those who use abuse to control their relationships: accusing someone else of the negative qualities they themselves embody.

Covert gaslighting is extremely insidious, destructive, and evil. It's a form of abuse that's even more dangerous than overt manipulation because it uses intense psychological torment to create chaos, confusion, and feelings of guilt, coupled with a sense of unreality—and all this within a supposedly God-sanctioned relationship. The covert abuser is extremely manipulative, full of contradictions and lies. For example, at times he'll appear caring and loving, and will do little things to show how well he's taking care of you, yet in the next moment he'll batter you with put-downs that cause your self-esteem to crumble. These criticisms are often so crafty and subtle that you're not fully aware of them, yet still you feel terrible and deflated even though you're not sure why. He'll talk in confusing circles until you're too exhausted to even understand what he's saying, then blame you for not communicating properly (in other words, in the way he specifies and demands), and for not listening attentively enough.

The tactic here is to continue to gaslight you, to try to convince you that your memory is failing. As the abuse progresses, you begin to wonder: *Could he be telling the truth? Should I go to the doctor, or take more fish oil pills for my memory? What's wrong with me? Am I really losing it? I tried so hard ... but maybe he's right ... he's so great to put up with me ....*

Once you realize what's going on, it becomes easier to see through these lies. Keep reminding yourself that this is exactly what's being fed to you—*lies*. "Lying lips are an abomination to the LORD" (Prov. 12:22).

"More Subtle Than Any of the Beasts of the Earth"

Back to the first abuser, the serpent, and to the evils of manipulation. As mentioned, covert tactics can be difficult to recognize, and even more difficult to admit as a problem in your relationship. How can you reconcile your "knight in shining armor" with the serpent? How can you admit that his armor isn't shining and glorious, but is rusted and full of dents?

The problem with a knight in shining armor is that you can't see what's behind all that impenetrable metal.

Here are some things to remember.

The person who employs covertly abusive tactics in order to gain control, to hide their core shame and vulnerability, and to maintain power over their spouse appears, to the outside world, like the nicest man in the world. Kind, caring, loving husband; these are characteristics he seeks to show others. He likely doesn't think of himself as acting abusively but thinks of himself as a decent guy (or even a great guy) who sometimes loses control and gets a bit too mad—but that's it. And only from time to time. In general, he's awesome. The abuse cycle isn't something he recognizes, or even knows about (without a decent dose of self-education, most victims don't recognize or know about this cycle, either). To outsiders, and even to family members other than his intimate partner, the covert aggressor appears humble, giving, supportive and even approachable. Only his spouse endures the destructive characteristics of his rage-filled, coercive behaviors. Dr. George Simon, Jr. calls these types of people "wolves in sheep's clothing,"[14] drawing upon Jesus' warning: "Beware of false prophets, who come to you in sheep's clothing but inwardly are ravenous wolves. You will know them by their fruits" (Matt 7:15-16).

These "wolves in sheep's clothing" are those subtle abusers who are the most manipulative, whether they act intentionally or not. Recall the biblical description of the serpent who was "more subtle than any other wild creature that the LORD God had made" (Gen 3:1). The Hebrew word for "serpent" is *nāhāsh,* a word that can describe any creature from a worm to a dragon. Interestingly, the same word is used in Isaiah 27:1 "to describe the great 'dragon' known as 'Leviathan the twisting serpent,' who was considered the embodiment of evil and chaos."[15] In other words, the worm can grow wings and become a fire-breathing dragon; he can manipulate in both covert and overt ways. In Revelation 12:9 the serpent of Genesis is identified as Satan, whom Jesus called the "father of lies" (John 8:44).

This is why abuse can legitimately be called evil. Again, I'm not accusing anyone of being demonic at the core of their innermost selves. We're all made in the image of God, and our true selves reflect His image. It's when a person fails to live within their true, God-given image—and instead live in a part of themselves that reflect volatile emotions and dangerous traits—that the serious issues occur.

---

[14] George Simon, Jr., Ph.D., *In Sheep's Clothing: Understanding and Dealing with Manipulative People, Revised Edition* (Little Rock, AR: Parkhurst Brothers, Inc., 2010).

[15] John Bergsma and Brant Pitre, *A Catholic Introduction to the Bible, Volume I: The Old Testament* (San Francisco, CA: Ignatius Press, 2018), 105.

That's why it's so important to separate evil people from evil deeds. Just because someone does evil things doesn't make them a chronically evil person. However, what I am emphatically stating is that abuse, itself, is an evil act—in all its categories and forms. This is something we must be absolutely firm about, and not excuse away under any minimizing secular talk of "disordered" or even merely "cruel." Yes, abusive behavior is disordered and unjustly cruel. But it also, and primarily, reeks of the stench of evil.

In Genesis 3:1-7, the serpent used the manipulative ploy of gaslighting to entice Eve through his half-truths. Anything that is not the full truth (including acts of omission) is a lie.

Satan told Eve that if she disobeyed God and ate of the tree of the knowledge of good and evil she wouldn't die as God had claimed (3:4). In other words, the father of lies twisted the truth, blame-shifting and projecting, accusing God of being the very thing that he himself is—a consummate liar. "For God knows that when you eat of it your eyes will be opened, and you will be like God, knowing good and evil" (3:5), the serpent claimed. Instead, after being manipulated into disobeying God, Eve became familiar with the fog of sin and corruption. She became less like God, not more.

Yet what Satan claimed ("you shall not die") seemed to be the truth, since Adam and Eve didn't physically die immediately after eating of the fruit. Does that mean Satan was the truthful one? Most certainly not. In fact, Jesus attests that Satan was "a murderer from the beginning" (John 8:44). This means that from the beginning, Adam and Eve did die—at the hands of Satan himself.

It was Satan's lies that caused a form of spiritual death, a death God had warned our first parents about—and it also introduced decay and eventual physical death into God's perfect world. Because they fell for the serpent's tricks, Adam and Eve caused a separation between themselves and God, introducing the corruption of original sin into the world.

"Do Not Fear Those Who Can Kill the Body But Cannot Kill the Soul …"

Comparing the tale of the serpent's deadly trickery to the sin of abuse may seem harsh to some, but it's accurate and helpful. Although sin and evil are topics that are often avoided and discarded in today's world, we can't hide from the fact that abuse is a grave sin. St. Thomas Aquinas wrote that "evil is the absence of the good that is natural and due to a thing … to sin is nothing else than to fail in the good which belongs to any being according to its nature."[16] The good that is natural and due to human beings is love, justice and the reflection of the "image and likeness of God" (Gen. 1:26) within our souls. Anything less is harmful at best, and ultimately destructive at worst. Abusive behavior causes corruption, just as Original Sin brought corruption into the world.

By his manipulative and evil tactics, the serpent was "a murderer from the beginning"; in comparison, abuse controls, thwarts, and attempts to murder the spirit. Even when an individual isn't purposely intending to "kill the spirit" of his loved one, if in his own

---

[16] St. Thomas Aquinas, *Summa Theologica I,* trans. the Fathers of the English Dominican Province. (1911, Reprint, Notre Dame, IN: Christian Classics, 1981), Q, 49, a. 1; St. Thomas Aquinas, *Summa Theologica I-II,* Q. 109, a. 2, ad. 2.

serious inner damage and need to control he's turning to abusive tactics, then he's doing just that. We can't think of such people as devils or evil personalities, because most likely they're not (true psychopaths and sociopaths are in a class by themselves, so I won't go there). Rather, these individuals are damaged, shame-filled human beings who are taking their damage out on their loved ones in the most unhealthy, devastating ways possible. Such people need to undergo a true conversion and healing, admit to their actions and motives, and seek professional help for their abusive inclinations.

Yet no matter how internally compromised a person is, we always need to remember one thing—*there is no excuse for abuse.* None whatsoever. The more someone tries to excuse his behavior and blame it on externals (his childhood, his parents, his siblings, his ex, stress at work, alcohol, you), the easier it is to see that he's not willing to let go of the control he seeks to have over you.

Abuse is the opposite of love, fidelity, devotion, and even life itself.

If we allow abuse to continue, we run the risk of it eventually killing our spirit. We must always remember that we're made in the image and likeness of God. We can't allow that image to be broken or even tarnished. We need to love ourselves, and God, more than that. Jesus told us to "Love your neighbor as yourself" (Mark 12:31), but these words presuppose that we authentically love ourselves. I'm not talking about the pompous self-love and selfish affirmations such as those that are so commonly taught in today's secular self-help books, but loving ourselves with authentic, Christ-driven charity. "Love is patient, love is kind …" (1 Cor. 13:4) We need to be patient with ourselves, and kind; and allowing ourselves to continue to be abused after we've recognized the destructive pattern in our marriages is not being kind to ourselves. We need change—one way or another, we need authentic change.

But more on that later. For now, I'll leave you with this: I believe that the key to love of self rests in Divine Mercy. "Be at peace, My child. See, you are not alone. My Heart watches over you," Jesus promised us through the vision of St. Faustina.[17] We have to trust Jesus, His forgiveness and His merciful love. This paves the way for trusting and loving ourselves.

Not remembering Jesus' Sacred Heart and the unyielding forgiveness He extends to us is like forgetting the sacrifice of the Cross. We have to allow ourselves love, forgiveness, and peace. Otherwise, we're not trusting in Jesus.

Jesus, I trust in You. Please help me to trust more.

---

[17] St. Maria Faustina Kowalska, *Diary of Saint Maria Faustina Kowalska,* trans. Adam and Danuta Pasicki and Archbishop George Pearce, S.M. (Stockbridge, MA: Association of Marian Helpers, 2012), 799.

Chapter Three

Verbal Attacks and Psychological Violence

"For every kind of beast and bird, or reptile and sea creature, can be tamed and has been tamed by mankind, but no human being can tame the tongue. It is a restless evil, full of deadly poison."

(James 3:7-8)

Have you been called cruel names by the person who is supposed to love you for who you are, as you are, "for better or for worse"? Some labels are overtly wounding, while other put-downs are more covert but no less hurtful. These can include such labels as:

- Impossible
- Irrational
- Difficult
- Useless
- Ridiculous
- A bad mother/spouse/person
- Mean
- Cold
- Confrontational
- Naïve
- Irresponsible
- And the list goes on … and on …

If any of this sounds familiar and is a consistent pattern in your relationship rather than an all-too-human "one-off" mistake, then you may be involved with an emotional abuser (emotional abuse includes psychological and verbal attacks). Think, too, about the context of the comments. If he claims he said things he "didn't mean" while refusing to admit the cruelty of his words, or if he claims to be the victim rather than perpetrator, be aware that these are major red flags.

Another tactic to look out for is comparing you to other people in his life—people he obviously resents—and attributing what he sees as their characteristics onto you. For example, maybe your spouse has mother issues; he dislikes his mother, sees her as a manipulative and emotionally cold woman, and says he's been damaged by her negative influence. Let's say that in one of his Mr. Hyde rages, he shouts in toxic anger, "You're the greatest manipulator since my mother!"

What then? Well, in context, you can realize what a damaged individual you're dealing with. He obviously has unresolved issues, but he should never take his psychological problems out on you. When hearing a phrase such as "You're the greatest manipulator since my mother," listening to it in context and knowing how he feels about his mother and her (real or imagined) manipulations sends a distinct and purposeful message to you. In this example he intends to more than "merely" zap yet another critical insult your way but is directly stating how he feels about you.

Solid relationships are built upon trust, mutual self-giving, friendship, and openness. All these things simply aren't possible with someone who can't see you for who you truly are, but rather views you through his own darkly-colored lens of distorted thinking, resentment, and past hurt (including injuries which have nothing to do with you).

"The good man out of the good treasure of his heart produces good, and the evil man out of his evil treasure produces evil; for out of the abundance of the heart his mouth speaks" (Luke 6:45).

There is No Excuse for Verbal Abuse

A manipulative and controlling personality will justify his abusive behaviors in any way he can. Twisted thinking, circular reasoning, and entitled attitudes all merge to create a wealth of excuses and blame. Abusers often believe they can get away with anything and sadly, they often do. Their tangled logic is mind-boggling and confusing, so it's important to understand how distorted this way of thinking can be. For example, an abuser will often excuse his behavior with twisted rationalizations, convinced that he can call his partners whatever he wants—as long as he also feels it's true.

Someone with unbalanced egoistic tendencies and a fondness for controlling his partner often uses this justification to violate his relationship through verbal attacks. "It's okay to call her stupid, because she truly *is* stupid!" he'll reason. The attacks then continue, and likely intensify. After all, his conscience has been appeased through his own unreasonable reasonings.

The tongue is a small member, yet it boasts of great things. How great a forest is set ablaze by such a small fire! And the tongue is a fire, a world of unrighteousness. The tongue is set among our members, staining the whole body, setting on fire the entire course of life (James 3:5-6).

A victim is often so engrossed in trying to figure out what she's doing wrong in her relationship—focusing on what she hopes she can do to make things better and how she can communicate on a deeper and more understandable level—that her own thinking gets tossed about until it twists into an unreasonable mass. This is a direct result of the confusion created by domestic abuse.

Verbal abuse is nasty, dehumanizing, cruel, and psychologically destructive. Anyone who advocates any form of verbal violence needs to rethink their attitudes, beliefs, and treatment of others.

And as I've said before, and will keep on saying—there is no excuse for abuse. In this case, there is *no excuse for any form of verbal abuse.*

Psychological Physical Abuse

Another violent tactic that's as commonly misunderstood as verbal abuse is that of psychological physical abuse. Many women don't realize they've been physically abused if they haven't been punched, strangled, kicked, threatened with a weapon, or beaten in any other way.

Yet this isn't so.

The most obvious tactics are easier to spot, yet physical abuse can come in a variety of forms. If a person threatens violence in order to intimidate, terrorize, and control his partner, he's committing a covert form of physical abuse. Even if he doesn't touch her, he's still being physically aggressive.

I call this *psychological physical violence (PPV)*.

Many manipulative personalities use the tactic of PPV to forcefully coerce a partner into submission. This type of intimidation can take the form of damaging property by punching holes in walls, breaking furniture, or throwing items across the room so they dramatically smash to pieces. An abuser may purposely destroy electronics, precious ornaments, photographs, or other items of emotional value, or attack pets. Picking locks to get at their target is another common tactic, as is violently slamming doors, especially when it causes the door or doorframe to crack and splinter.

Using PPV has many advantages for the abuser. It allows him to physically attack and terrorize his victim without feeling the shame of laying a hand on her or having to look at the bruises he created. Quite often his excuse for his excessive behavior is "I was just blowing off steam" or "this is how all guys act when they're upset." (Notice the minimizing language that's so typical of manipulators— merely "blowing off steam" rather than raging, and "upset" rather than "infuriated.")

Is he right? Do all guys punch holes in walls, hurl objects across the room, or kick the cat when they need to "blow off steam"?

Definitely not. These are actions of an enraged abusive personality, not of someone with a healthy and justified anger which can be resolved through open and loving communication.

Another advantage psychological physical violence has for the perpetrator is that it sends a clear and definite message, without having to say a word. *I'm capable of violence. I'm stronger than you, more powerful than you, and I can do serious damage if I want.*

If you're on the receiving end of this type of abuse, you may find yourself in a double-bind. On the one hand you're terrified, and each incident instills yet more terror. The result of prolonged exposure to this sort of violence is often severe yet generalized fear, anxiety, and even panic attacks. PTSD settles in and sets up living space within you. Every sharp, loud, or unexpected noise makes you jump. You tremble, you fear. Life is foggy, hazy, surreal.

Yet you've never been physically hurt, so at the same time you may feel a sense of gratitude. *Well, at least it's not that bad,* you may think, minimizing the truth in order to cope. *It could be worse ...*

But please be aware. It may very well get worse—violence usually does, unless an abusive person experiences a complete conversion and determines to turn his life around (which happens, but is rare—more on that in chapter nine).

If you're still entangled with your abuser, be vigilant and alert (1 Peter 5:8). Where there's PPV, actual physical violence is lurking sulkily around the corner—bruises and broken bones and perhaps even worse.

Be aware. Get help. Find a reliable and trustworthy support system, both professionally and personally. Above all, create a safety plan. Even if you think you'll never need it (and hopefully you're right), a safety plan can save your life. Information on safety planning can be found in the appendix.

Abuse of any kind nearly always accelerates the more the cycle of manipulation spins. The periods between "bait/adoration" and "tension build-up/explosion" get shorter and shorter as the weeks, months, years and even decades go by.

If you're experiencing psychological physical violence, take this as a red flag that the next time his fist may be aimed at you rather than the wall. If you're afraid this may happen, even though it never has before, trust your intuition, which most often comes from the Holy Spirit, the still small Voice within (1 Kings 19:12). There are people out there who love you and support you, no matter where you may find yourself today. Even if you currently feel the dread of hopelessness, please know that your situation is not hopeless. Reach out. Seek, and you will find.

"He heals the brokenhearted and binds up their wounds" (Ps. 147:3).

Is it Child Abuse if the Mother is Abused, but Not the Child?

As I was writing this chapter, one of my newsletter subscribers sent me an email describing how her ex-husband, when they were still married and their children were young, used to love playing the Rolling Stones song "Under My Thumb" as often as he could, laughing in a tauntingly cruel way. He'd encourage his children to sing along as if he was playing a carefree, fun game with them. They often did exactly what their dad wanted, not realizing how much they were wounding their mother. After all, they didn't know he was purposely tormenting her, and they simply wanted his approval—even if they did feel, deep down, that there was something cruel about what their father was doing.

This sent a double-message to the confused and vulnerable children. First, their father made it clear they'd only get approval from him if they went along with his "teasing," which sent the bewildering message that if they didn't antagonize their mother, they wouldn't get his admiration or love. They were also being taught that a woman's place was "under the thumb" of her superior husband.

This particular man never hit his kids. He never called them ugly, or stupid, or worthless. This means he never abused his children, only his intimate partner. Right?

No. Not right.

To abuse a child's parent is to abuse the child. Even if not in a direct and overt manner, this is still a form of emotional and psychological maltreatment. The trickle-down effect is enormous, extending far beyond childhood and potentially tainting future adult relationships. It's also important to remember that young children are cognitively incapable of understanding the abuse they witness against a parent as being separate from themselves, so their brains process the violence as if they are the ones who are the actual target. A child forced to live his or her most vulnerable years in such an environment is likely to bear a lifetime of wounds, unless they seek active healing.

Often the child of an abusive parent will unwittingly be used as a "flying monkey." Named after the hypnotized creatures in *The Wizard of Oz* who flew around fulfilling the evil errands of the Wicked Witch of the West, an abuser's flying monkeys act in concert with him to antagonize, wound, and stir up the intended target. Some flying monkeys are devoted to the manipulator and do his bidding without question, making themselves a sort of "co-abuser."

Others—such as innocent children—have no idea they're being brainwashed into complying with abuse. They fully believe what their parent tells them because, after all, parents are to be trusted. Or so a child thinks.

It's cruel to turn a child into a flying monkey, and it creates enormous psychological turmoil within the developing brain. On the one hand, the child desperately wants to please her abusive parent and gain approval (not realizing, of course, that the parent is manipulating the entire family). On the other hand, the child intuitively knows something is amiss.

It's obviously wrong to insist someone isn't very smart, is naïve, useless, cold, ugly, or controlling, yet if a beloved and trusted parent is saying those things about the other parent, then what's a child to think—let alone do?

A child who has never heard of "cognitive dissonance" and wouldn't understand the phrase even if it was said to them can still understand the effects of such extreme psychological and emotional trauma.

This brainwashing—one parent convincing a child that their other parent is a monster, a liar, a cheater, an idiot, inexperienced, rigid, or just plain wrong (or whatever preferred labels are used)—tends to taint the parent-child relationship well after the child becomes an adult. One victim of this type of childhood abuse recently confessed to me:

It was a difficult thing for me to admit to myself, but for three decades—until my father's mask slipped and I saw him for the abusive man he is—I believed his lies. He convinced my siblings and I that my mother was too naïve to be able to make good decisions, too stupid to raise us properly (even though, in actuality, she raised us single-handedly, with little help from him). We were taught to view a highly intelligent, loving, open-minded woman as silly and forgetful, controlling and closed-minded.

And I believed it. I believed all the lies. I've always loved my mother, but I certainly didn't respect her. I'd been brainwashed. After all, she was a bit ditzy. And she admitted it! *Because she, too, had been brainwashed by him.* I realize that now. I realize it all now!

It's difficult to break free from such deeply ingrained gaslighting. After all, I trusted my dad. I never imagined he'd lie to me—especially in such a harsh way.

Yet evil is always exposed. Cruelty can live long, but not forever. Admitting the truth is harsh, yet so freeing, even after 33 years.

Healing from the manipulative brainwashing caused by this type of child abuse takes great effort and a conscious adjustment of thought. It requires an honest assessment and an uncritical look at the past. For the adult child of an emotionally abusive parent, coming to terms with that parent's manipulative personality and realizing that one's own perceptions, beliefs and experiences of the past have been built on a series of progressively brutal lies can be a harsh reality to take in. Yet it's a reality that must be admitted if true healing is to be accomplished.

Facing these difficult truths can also break generational abuse. Children of toxic parents often end up marrying similar spouses, because that type of personality is familiar and even comfortable to them. They've been conditioned to accept mistreatment as "normal"—and therefore they don't recognize a manipulative personality when they engage with one.

Other victimized children grow up to become abusive themselves. They act what they know, and they perpetuate the sad cycle.

It's time to take control: of our lives, ourselves, our memories and perceptions, and of our ability to authentically love—without borders or boundaries, without any controlling strings or conditions attached.

By facing the truth, we face healing. We end the cycle and create a nurturing environment so the next generation can flourish in faith, hope, love, and peace.

Chapter Four

Pride of Place: Why Isolation is So Common in Abusive Relationships

"Although it is often largely unconscious, abusive men are aware on some level that a woman's social contacts can bring her strength and support that could ultimately enable her to escape his control. An abusive man commonly attempts to keep his partner dependent on him to increase his power."

(Lundy Bancroft, *Why Does He Do That?*)

Extreme jealousy—often taking the form of possessiveness and overbearing social restrictions—is common in abusive relationships. This tactic of manipulation can take many forms, all with an end goal of isolating the target from the outside world. Whether consciously or not, the individual who uses abuse to control his relationship wants to keep his partner to himself, to ensure she's available whenever he wishes, in whatever way he desires. He may also have a strong need to reassure himself that she'll never leave, since many individuals who use abusive approaches to their relationship do so out of a desperate fear of abandonment.

If you maintain close relationships with anyone other than your partner, he'll likely feel his control slipping. After all, being around other people may cause you to reassess your situation and therefore to be less vulnerable to his gaslighting, criticisms, and influence. External friendships will help you maintain a higher level of self-esteem and self-worth. And, if you're exposed to other couples, you may see what a healthy relationship looks like—and begin to question your own.

Although an abuser may not consciously harbor these thoughts, the underlying attitudes are still present.

If you're in an unhealthy relationship yet have managed to maintain social connections, your ability to nourish close ties with other people likely causes your spouse a high level of insecurity. Outside relationships give him less control over you, and it also means your attentions aren't focused on him 24/7—something an abusive personality cannot tolerate.

Excessive jealousy gives him a suspicious, anger-filled need to frequently check up on you when you're out of his physical grasp. He may hide his true motives behind a mask of "I love you" and "I just want to be sure you're safe," which would naturally cause you to feel cherished and protected. You're blindsided into submission, not realizing that this sort of "protection" is not only false but also dangerous to your wellbeing.

How does a manipulative person accomplish his goal of isolation (again, whether conscious or not)? It takes a series of progressive steps, steps that cause you to slowly adapt to the "new normal" of his increasing control until, before you're even aware of it, you're living the life he mandates. For example, you may suddenly realize—years later—that your own life has dripped away, piece by piece, most often without you even realizing what was happening.

This occurs slowly. First you feast on his words of encouragement, unity, and solidarity—words you take to heart, trusting the good intentions. "I'm so happy when you succeed," "I'll totally support whatever you want to do," "I hope you have a fun evening with your friends." Yet when you return home from the gym or a career seminar, time with friends or dinner with colleagues, you're grilled with distressing questions about where you've been and what you did. And no answer you give—regardless of how honest and innocent your words may be—is enough to satisfy him. Somehow, you're still to blame, somehow you still did something wrong. *But what?*

His previous words of affirmation turn to dust, and you're left confused and deflated. You did the best you could. He encouraged you ... He supported you ... But then ...

No matter what your response, you're barraged by verbal, emotional, and perhaps even physical abuse.

Or, he may say he supports your career, but then he proceeds to sabotage it by frequently interrupting your sleep (with fights, coercive demands for sex, or other attacks). He may constantly call you at work or even stop by your office, interrupting important tasks or meetings. Because of the stress of your relationship and his constant demands, you might end up performing poorly at your job, perhaps even losing it through quitting (lack of self-esteem and his insistence that he'll take care of you) or being fired (because of his controlling persistence and invasive interruptions).

Those are merely two examples out of many, but you get the idea.

An abuser will say one thing yet do another, sowing confusion and doubt within the mind of his target, causing her to feel as if she's developing dementia or going crazy.

Just what he wants.

If you've ever felt this way, be assured—you're not crazy, and you don't need your head checked. You've just been a victim of gaslighting and his distorted belief patterns, but the effects can be reversed. You can get your life back. Educating yourself and becoming aware of the tactics he's been using is the first major step.

If you think about it, you may realize that your spouse has progressively isolated you by saying negative and critical things about your friends, family, hobbies, or the places you enjoy visiting. His words are so convincing that you wonder if he may be right. Before you know it—and without even being aware of how it happened—you may find yourself sharing his opinions. Why had you ever wanted to hang out with those people, anyway? Why had you wanted to go to those places, or enjoy those things? If you're in this position, you may not be able to remember any longer.

It's safer to do things with him, and him alone. Staying at home in isolation is safer, too. If you stay at home, you won't expose yourself to potential toxins—mainly the toxin of his psychological and verbal abuse. If you distance yourself socially from your family and friends, you won't have to run the risk of offending your partner. Life will be far more comfortable if you just give in and "go with the flow."

In numb despair you may be convinced there's no purpose in trying to stand up to him. He has too much power. So you succumb, because it's easier and less stressful that way, and you have enough stress as it is. Avoiding conflict has likely become your top priority.

And, chances are, isolation has become your habit and trap. You may feel alone, withdrawn, and lonely because it seems the world around you has changed. You're no longer comfortable—not in your own skin, not in your own life, not in your own world.

This is the true face of abuse: Being brainwashed into thinking the world isn't safe, so you have to distance yourself. Being led to believe that if you get close to another human being, you're in danger. Being told you cannot live, unless you live with your abuser, who will keep you safe.

Even though he's the one instigating all the evil in your life.

This, my friends, is coercive control. This, my friends, is the true face of abuse. Whether on a personal or global level, *this is abuse.*

An Insidious Agenda: Isolating Targets from Family

Isolation is particularly toxic if your partner encourages you to withdraw from your family.

Abusers often use manipulative tactics to slowly isolate their targets from the loving support of family in much the same way as they try to isolate their targets from everyone else. Some ways your partner may do this include (but aren't limited to):

- He'll lie about your loved ones, claiming they said or did something behind your back that was unkind, dismissive, or demeaning. Because you still trust your husband, you believe him, and consequently doubts about your family begin to creep into your mind. Slowly, imperceptibly, a divide between yourself and your supportive loved ones begins to form.

- Your partner acts in embarrassing ways in front of your family, causing you deep humiliation and creating a hesitation to join future family gatherings. This can include getting inappropriately drunk, dominating the conversation with pompous self-talk, making snide and cutting comments about you in front of everyone, or belittling other family members. This creates a distinctly uncomfortable feeling for everyone, yet it may be so vague no one is quite sure what's wrong.

- In private, he may put your family down and point out their shortcomings—whether real, imagined, or grossly exaggerated. If you still have faith in your husband's "honesty," you may find yourself taking his words to heart and may even be gaslit into thinking he knows better than you do (because you've been told you're "naïve," or "unobservant," or whatever label he finds most effective). Slowly, before you even realize what's happening, your opinion of your family begins to erode. You view them as flawed, irritating, a bad influence on your relationship, or whatever projection your partner wants to implant within you.

- He may act extremely charming toward the important people in your life, causing them to love and admire him, while subtly putting you down in front of everyone. The humiliation is too much to bear, so eventually you'd rather skip family time than face the shame you feel because of his covert lies.

- He claims it's extremely uncomfortable for him to be around your family because they dislike him or treat him unfairly (for example, he may falsely accuse them of looking down on him because of his career, religion, political outlook, physical appearance, etc.). In reality, it could be that they don't like him because they can see him for who he is.

Another manipulative trick is to get the target to believe *you* are the one who made the decision to stay away from your loved ones. After all, he never overtly forbade you to visit your parents, siblings, or friends.

If any of this sounds familiar, and you've realized you're a victim of isolation, remember that it was his actions and lies about your friends and family that drove you to self-isolate. Chances are his tactics were so crafty you couldn't see them for what they were—and consequently you may be blaming yourself. This creates immense confusion. Domestic violence experts John Gottman and Neil Jacobson recount the following victim testimony in their book *When Men Batter Women: New Insights Into Ending Abusive Relationships*:

> I gradually took on these opinions as if they were my own and after a while lost all of my friends. My husband never really told me that I couldn't see them, but he was so effective at convincing me that they were slime that I didn't want to see them. So, soon I had no friends, and I didn't feel that I could directly blame my husband for that. But I came to feel like it was just the two of us, alone on a desert island. I was

as lonely as I would have been if we were the only two people on the planet.[18]

You may have even come to the realization that your spouse has isolated you from your own children—both young children and those who are adults. Children are a particular threat to most abusers because a mother's connection to them can be her main—and often only—source of joy, fulfilment, and strength. By damaging the mother-child relationship, the abuser is able to gain a fuller level of control and power over his entire family (this is true regardless of whether or not the abuser is the biological father of the children). Typical methods of mother/child isolation include (but again, aren't limited to):

- He may belittle you in front of your children by telling them you're flighty, controlling, naïve, not as intelligent as him, or any other form of diminishment.
- Convincing the kids that he's the "fun one" and you're mean, controlling, or too much of an authoritarian.
- Undermining your parenting by encouraging the kids to break household rules. After all, you're too rigid and controlling—and he's the fun one!
- Slandering you to your children by falsely accusing you of being a spendthrift, of flirting/cheating, or betraying him in some other way.

---

[18] Gottman and Jacobson, *When Men Batter Women*, 152.

- Convincing the children that you neglect him—and them— and that you don't truly love them. You aren't a good mother or aren't attentive enough, according to his abusive standards. But he, of course, is all-attentive and wonderful.
- He may damage your ability to parent by criticizing you, calling you names, or making cruel "jokes" about you.
- If the children are adults, he may force limitations on the time you spend with them, claiming you're being too clingy and need to "just let go."

Again, this list may look familiar since the techniques are so common in exploitative relationships. Isolation leads to extreme loneliness, which in turn has likely caused you to cling to the only person now in your life—your abuser. This is by design (whether consciously or not) and strengthens the trauma bond as well as increases your spouse's control over your life.

Domestic abuse sends a clear psychological message: *It's scary out there in the big bad world!* This tactic works, and it works well. When isolation is solidly entrenched, you may find you've become so socially distant that you no longer know how to conduct yourself around others.

You cling to your isolation as if it'll protect you, yet it's the primary thing that's keeping you from healing. Even when change is being made—firm boundaries are put in place, or you leave—even then, the habit of isolation feels too safe to release.

Yet this step is necessary. God made us social creatures (Gen. 2:18). The healthy support of others is a crucial component to healing. A loving touch, a kind word, a generous hug, genuine companionship—those are the things that make us human. When anyone tries to take that from us, they're robbing us of our God-graced humanity.

Always keep in mind that abuse is an attempt by one party to coercively manipulate another into submission, thereby taking away their independence, freedom, individuality, and humanity. This is the humanity God gave us. We can't let His gift be controlled by another.

Healthy and loving relationships are necessary to regain a sense of safety and trust in the world—and in the self. The habit of isolation needs to be broken, even if the idea seems terrifying at first. Knowing you're safe—with safe people—is a critical component of healing. This rewires the trauma-damaged brain and helps develop a renewed capacity to feel independent, competent, and cherished within a loving community.

While the support of true family and friends is crucial, it's also helpful to find ways to connect with fellow survivors. A spiritual support group that incorporates elements of healthy healing through the guidance of the Holy Spirit and reassurance of Sacred Scripture can be of particular benefit. Such a group can help renew and rejuvenate faith, hope and love—in self, in God, in others, and in the world. No one is truly alone, even when it seems that way. "Fear not, for I am with you, be not dismayed, for I am your God; I will strengthen you, I will help you, I will uphold you with My victorious right hand" (Isa. 41:10).

Why Prolonged Abuse Keeps You Locked in a FOG

In addition to isolation, prolonged abuse causes a hazy brain-fog that seems to settle over not only your mind, but your entire self—body, spirit, and innermost depths.

Physically you may feel depleted, exhausted, and perhaps even in actual pain. A few of the most common effects of chronic abuse include headaches, achy joints or muscles, and stomach issues. An erratic heartbeat or palpitations are also typical physical symptoms, as are shortness of breath, dizziness, generalized anxiety, sleep disturbances (either too much or not enough), and cognitive confusion.

Emotionally you may feel flattened and defeated or—as I heard one young adult recently describe her victimized mother—*crumpled and broken.* Spiritually you may have lost joy, connection, optimism, and the ability to feel the fullness of life.

You've lost faith, hope, and love. And when the greatest of these things has proven to be the most destructive, where does that leave you?

You likely feel distanced—from friends and family, from what was once the richness of your spiritual life, from yourself.

From your true, innermost self.

You may not even remember who your true self had once been, or perhaps you wonder if you ever knew her in the first place.

Domestic abuse causes a horrific dismantling of personhood, piece by piece and bit by bit, until the fog is so thick you fear you'll never be able to make your way through it. This fogginess becomes so impenetrable it seems impossible to move beyond its confining layers.

What are the key tactics abusers use to create this debilitating fog? As best-selling author, therapist, and speaker Dr. Susan Forward puts it, this fog is created by ...

Well, *FOG*.

Fear, obligation, and guilt.[19]

- *Fear.* As someone who has endured months, years, even decades of relationship abuse, you're likely afraid to do anything that will trigger your spouse's next "Mr. Hyde" episode (even though it's impossible to predict what that "something" might be). You're afraid to disagree with him, to express your own opinions or to reveal your true self. You tend to creep around your own home, carefully watching what you say, do, and even think. You may find yourself prone to anxiety or panic attacks, or random feelings of fear that seem to have no connection to anything immediately going on in your day. Sadly, all this has become a way of life for you.

- *Obligation.* You likely feel obligated to give in to your abuser's demands, standards, and beliefs. He's brainwashed you into feeling this sense of obligation and has convinced you it's a way of showing him respect and love. Besides, life

---

[19] Susan Forward, Ph.D., *Emotional Blackmail: When the People in Your Life Use Fear, Obligation and Guilt to Manipulate You* (NY, NY: HarperCollins, 1997), xi.

is easier to just give in, and slightly less tumultuous. *But only slightly.*

- **Guilt.** Guilt weighs heavily against your shoulders—but unbeknownst to you, it's been put there by your abuser, to make you comply to his incessant demands. You don't even realize that it's *his* voice replaying in your head, telling you how you've failed, how you should be doing better, how he is so much more loving and supportive and adequate than you are, how you don't give enough or love enough or … how you simply *aren't* enough. You don't realize that your guilty thoughts have been implanted—by him.

Clearing the fog so you can rebuild your life is crucial. But how do you begin?

Even if you're still involved with your abuser, you can take fruitful and life-saving steps forward.

Talk, share, don't keep it all inside. Find someone you can trust—an empathetic friend, family member, spiritual director, therapist, group—and *talk*. Then talk some more. Minimizing your trauma by pretending that everything is fine does more damage than good. All isn't well, and facing the truth is the first step toward your new future. The sooner you can acknowledge that, the sooner the fog will start to lift and healing can begin.

Pray without ceasing *(1 Thess 5:17).* This is the one thing that can bring you the most peace and clarity, no matter where you're at on your spiritual journey—but sadly, it can also be the most difficult.

Domestic abuse has likely zapped you of everything—especially your spiritual connection, a connection which bridges the gap between your true, innermost self and the external trauma being thrown at you from all angles. It's essential to heal your entire being, especially your soul. It's essential to repair that bridge.

Go slow. Don't put pressure on yourself. To "pray without ceasing" seems intimidating and impossible, but it's actually not. You don't have to live in a secluded convent or find a solitary cave so you can pray 24/7. God doesn't expect that. We all have real lives, and our lives exist in the world God created, not solely on a picturesque mountaintop or dwelling in a secluded yurt.

What "pray without ceasing" actually means is that in order to live your fullest life, you need to release everything to Divine will—into God's hands, in the care of the Holy Spirit. Remember God's presence and grace in your life and remember it constantly.

No one can travel this path in isolation—and, happily, you don't have to navigate by yourself. "Ask, and it shall be given" (Matt 7:7).

This means asking for help, support, for a spiritual reconnection to something greater than yourself, and for God to open doors you never thought possible.

"Seek, and you shall find." Release your self-pressure and expectations. Rest, heal, understand. And then, eventually—when you're ready—act within the new life that will open up for you. But first, rest some more.

You deserve rest. And you need it.

Write it out. Keeping a journal is particularly crucial if you're still involved in your abusive relationship, yet tremendously healing no matter where you're at in your life. Journaling will help you gain greater clarity and insight, allow you to vent justifiable anger, frustration and sorrow in a healthy way, and will also derail future gaslighting. When your abuser says or does something he later denies and tells you you're crazy for even thinking he'd say/do such a thing, it's easy to doubt yourself and believe him. Yet if you can look back at your journal and find proof that he's again lying and trying to gaslight you, the gas suddenly gets turned off.

You can also use journaling to detect patterns in the abuse cycle, which can be immensely helpful and eye-opening. The progression of abuse can be documented, and returning to entries weeks, months, even years later can give you greater insight and clarity into your situation. This in turn will help you seek the strength you need to change your circumstances, if you haven't done so already. If you have, you'll find an even deeper level of healing. When you keep a journal, you can be honest with yourself in ways you normally wouldn't dare. This is so incredibly crucial.

A word of caution, however: If you fear your abuser will find your journal, if feel you need to be careful, go with your gut instinct. Hide your writing someplace he'd never discover it, have a trusted friend keep it for you, or whatever else you need to do to maintain your safety. Even if he's never before been physically abusive toward you, if you're afraid, there's a reason for your fear. *Trust yourself.*

Start tuning in to your intuition. That "still small voice" of your Spirit-guided intuition is still there, even if it seems like it's vanished. Your inner wisdom hasn't been obliterated, only muffled.

It's time to unwrap the muffler and start listening. This will take time and patience, because chronic self-doubt is one of the most common consequences of being abused. Slowly, as the fog lifts and your confidence increases, you'll begin to remember how to listen to that "small still voice" dwelling inside you, that internal compass of wisdom, compassion, and strength (1 Kings 19:12).

Remember, brain fog consists of your abuser's voice, not the truth. The words, gaslighting, brainwashing, and crazy-making are all lies thrown at you to dismantle your inner self, keep you off-balance, and make you easier to control. All this works—but doesn't have to be permanent.

It's understandable if you fear loss, rejection, financial instability, his anger, or *him* in general. You may feel obligated to be a good wife, to be attentive and loving at all times, to support him in every way, even to the detriment of yourself. In particular, you've been taught to be empathetic toward his "issues" and "wounds" (covert abusers love to play the victim). Yet these are *his* imposed obligations, rules and issues, *his* voice, and *his* demands. Separate the *his* from the *yours* in a loving, non-accusatory way. Find your true self, as God intended you to be, and act accordingly. In the words of St. Catherine of Siena, "If you are who you were meant to be, you'll set the world on fire!"[20]

Guilt is a heavy burden—and one that abusers love to encourage. If you feel guilty, you're easy to control. You may feel guilty that you didn't do enough for him or the relationship, that you didn't support

---

[20] St. Catherine of Siena, *The Letters of Catherine of Siena, Volume IV*, trans. Suzanne Noffke, O.P. (Tempe, AZ: Arizona Center for Medieval and Renaissance Studies, 2008), Letter T368, 320.

him enough, you didn't show enough affection, you're not a good enough mother or wife or person or friend.

Remember, these are all blame-shifting tactics he uses to exert more control over you and to manipulate you into behaving the way he wants. The fog in your head is *him* in your head. When you begin to consciously renounce his claims over you to make room for your own voice and your true self, authentic healing can start to unfold and enrich your life.

Chapter Five

Assaulting the Sacred:
Sexual Coercion in the Marriage Bed

"[Lustful] desire has the effect that in the interior, in the 'heart' …
it tramples on the ruins of the spousal meaning of the body …
it aims directly toward one and only one end as its object:
to satisfy only the body's sexual urge."

(St. Pope John Paul II, *Theology of the Body*, 40:4)

Trigger warning: If you're a victim of sexual abuse and haven't yet healed from the trauma, this chapter may be difficult for you to read. If so, remember that self-care is crucial. Read slowly, at your own pace, only as you can tolerate—or skip the chapter entirely if it's too much for you right now.

Many women don't realize they've been victims of sexual abuse in their marriages. Tragically, rape and violent physical assaults can and do happen within committed relationships, but most often these crimes remain unreported and even unacknowledged. However, there are other forms of sexual abuse that are crucial to understand, and that's why in this chapter I'm focusing on the subtle and insidious manipulation of sexual coercion.

Sexual abuse takes many forms, and it's important to recognize them all. Just because you're married doesn't mean your husband has free reign over your body. In fact, that idea is very anti-biblical, since husbands are supposed to treat their wives with the utmost respect: "Husbands, love your wives, as Christ loved the Church and gave himself up for her ... husbands should love their wives as their own bodies. He who loves his wife loves himself" (Eph. 5:25,28). If a husband loves his wife as Christ loves the Church, then sexual abuse shouldn't even be a concern.

Yet it is, even in sacred, sacramental Catholic marriages. This type of abuse often mingles with spiritual abuse, with the claim that sexual intimacy is a "wifely duty." Often the lines from 1 Corinthians 7:4-5 are quoted out of context: "For the wife does not rule over her own body, but the husband does ... Do not refuse one another ..." This truncation of the chapter is a deliberate twisting of St. Paul's words, a way of abusing biblical verses in order to try to make them fit a certain agenda. The full lines of this passage read:

> But because of the temptation to immorality, each man should have his own wife and each woman her own husband. The husband should give to his wife her conjugal rights, and likewise the wife to her husband. For the wife does not rule over her own body, but the husband does; likewise the husband does not rule over his own body, but the wife does. Do not refuse one another except perhaps by agreement for a season, that you may devote yourselves to prayer, but then come together again, lest Satan tempt you through lack of self-control. I say this by way of a concession, not of a command (1 Cor. 7:2-6).

St. Paul wrote these lines to a Greek culture steeped in debauchery and awry sexual practices as a way of introducing the Christian truth of mutual self-giving in marriage, as well as to counter certain sects of Greek aesthetics who shunned marriage and all bodily physical pleasure (1 Tim. 4:1-3). He also insists on a wife's equal conjugal right within marriage. Some Gentiles in the ancient world believed the wife had to remain faithful to her husband, but the husband wasn't expected to stay faithful to his wife.[21] The insistence on mutual, unselfish sexual intimacy is the point of St. Paul's letter to the converts in Corinth, one he had to emphasize due to the habits of the culture. Again, he's insisting upon equality in a loving, committed relationship—not sexual coercion, manipulation, or power-over. Additionally, these teachings of Paul come directly after his reminder that our bodies are members of Christ and temples of the Holy Spirit, to be cherished and loved—not to be abused (1 Cor. 6:15,19).

Isolating certain lines in the Bible to fit a particular agenda is a manipulative tactic used by Satan, the father of lies (see Matt. 4:1-11). Chapter six deals with more biblical misconceptions, including Jesus' teaching on forgiving seventy times seven (Matt. 18:21-22) and the true meaning of Ephesians 5.

The Alarm-Clock Method of Sexual Coercion

Sexual assault isn't limited to physical force or initially agreeing to a sexual encounter but later saying no, yet he refuses to stop.

---

[21] Craig S. Keener, commentary on 1 Corinthians 7 in *NIV Cultural Backgrounds Study Bible: Bringing to Life the Ancient World of Scripture*, ed. Craig S. Keener and John H. Walton (Grand Rapids, MI: Zondervan, 2016), 1993.

Those few examples show obvious, overt sexual abuse. But what about the covert assaults?

Sexual coercion is just one example of what hidden sexual abuse may look like, but hopefully this one example will help you understand that assaults upon the sacred body should never be tolerated. We need to name these assaults for what they are—lust, sin, and degradation of a human being.

In other words, evil.

Before I describe an example of what sexual coercion can look like, I want to mention a few other methods of intimate manipulation that are in no way acceptable, and are all forms of abusive, selfish behavior on the part of the offender. These include:

- Self-focused disregard for your wants, needs, level of exhaustion or health (both physical and emotional health).
- Frequently using sex as a bargaining tool. "If you have sex with me, I'll … (fill in the blank).
- Threatening sinful and adulterous behavior if his carnal demands aren't met. He may say something like, "Men have needs. If you're not willing, I'll have to go elsewhere," or he may blame you for his pornography addiction, claiming your "inattention" or "coldness" led him to seek his own way of release. These excuses are classic cases of blame-shifting, manipulation, and extreme abuse.
- If you feel degraded during a sexual encounter with your spouse, and you can't talk to him with understanding and empathy about how you feel, this is abuse. It's estimated that 40 to 45 percent of verbally and emotionally abusive

relationships also include sexual abuse,[22] and an even higher percentage include hidden sexual addictions such as pornography (I write more about the infidelity of pornography later in this chapter). When deviant sexual behaviors are a part of your partner's life, this often infiltrates your marriage bed in demeaning ways, such as demanding certain uncomfortable actions or performances.

- It's common for abusers to be highly jealous and to accuse their partners of their own misbehaviors—especially infidelity. (Infidelity isn't limited to actual physical affairs—but more on that later.) If your husband unjustly accuses you of having an affair, and then claims you have to "prove" to him that you're not being unfaithful by engaging in unwanted sexual contact with him, this is abuse.

- If he consistently claims, "you started it, so you have to finish it," simply because you reached out in non-sexual affection such as wanting to hold his hand or put your arm around him, this is also another form of coercive manipulation and abuse.

As you can see, there are many ways to sexually coerce a partner, and all of them are degrading, unacceptable, and go against God's plan for a true, sacramental, and holy marriage.

As an example of what one common form of sexual coercion looks like, I'm going to focus on what I call the "alarm clock method

---

[22] See Jacquelyn C. Campbell and Karen L. Soeken, "Forced Sex and Intimate Partner Violence: Effects on Women's Risk and Women's Health," *Violence Against Women* 5, no. 9 (September 1999): 1017-35.

of sexual coercion"—when your spouse expects physical "intimacy" at regular intervals, with consequences if you don't wish to engage. This isn't love or intimacy—it's forced obligation. It's as if he believes you've lost your right to say no to him once you've said "I do"—and there are consequences if you don't wish to engage.

For example, he may demand sex every three or four days. If the allotted time goes by and his expectations aren't met, all hell breaks loose. "Hell" can be overt violence, or his tactics could be more covert.

The covert manipulations are exceptionally insidious because they're so baffling due to their subtly, causing you to feel as if perhaps you're going crazy, not being kind enough, making things up, or blowing a minor situation out of proportion (you're doing none of those things). Aggressors often take the form of victimhood: "Oh, poor me, you don't love me, you don't find me attractive, you hate me, I'm a man so I have certain needs …" etc. If you deny him sex for any reason—a headache/backache/any ache, exhaustion from a day with the kids, emotional exhaustion from a day with him, or for any other reason—you'll be blamed and labeled "cold" and "insensitive." This causes you, the victim of domestic abuse, to feel guilt along with empathy and love, and therefore to give in to his sexual coercion. This doesn't make you a co-partner in his sexual game; it makes you a forced victim, even though you weren't physically forced.

With covert abuse, you don't even realize you're being sexually assaulted. And that, perhaps, is most tragic of all.

If your husband insistently—yet not necessarily with a loud tone of voice or harsh words—pressures, harasses, or guilt-trips you until you eventually gives in not out of an intimate desire but out of a desire to make him stop his harassment, free choice is being taken away from you. This is particularly true since in most cases, there's usually an implied threat if you don't eventually cave in—either he'll keep badgering you, not letting you sleep until he gets his way, you'll get the silent treatment for the next few days, or an abusive explosion will eventually culminate if his efforts continue to be deflected. Regardless of the consequences, there will be consequences. And so you give in, to avoid even more discomfort.

That's sexual assault, not authentic intimacy.

Sexual intimacy with your husband is designed, by God, to be a sacred and even spiritual act of mutual self-giving. To make it otherwise is a perversion. That's why the Catholic Church has such a firm stance against infidelity, masturbation, pornography, and all the rest. Those things aren't love—in fact, they're one of the biggest offenses against our true human nature, made in the image and likeness of God Himself (Gen. 1:26).

Shun immorality. Every other sin which a man commits is outside the body; but the immoral man sins against his own body. Do you not know that your body is a temple of the Holy Spirit within you, which you have from God? ... So glorify God in your body" (1 Cor. 6:18-20).

Shun Immorality

This issue is so crucial—and so misunderstood—that I want to dive into it on a deeper level. Sexual coercion within marriages is a subject that needs to be brought fully into the light because it's sadly so common, yet you may not even recognize it. You might feel something is wrong, and experience heartbreak and frustration, but often you don't understand the source of your feelings and so may try to shrug them off or minimize them, especially if your husband has told you that you're "too sensitive" or you "blow things out of proportion."

Yet that's not true. Your deep sense of "something wrong" is your intuition—the voice of the Holy Spirit speaking to you from within. Listen, don't ignore. In the words of Pope Paul VI,

> a conjugal act imposed on one's spouse without regard to his or her condition, or personal and reasonable wishes in the matter, is no true act of love, and therefore offends the moral order in its particular application to the intimate relationship of husband and wife.[23]

Saint John Paul II wrote a masterwork on the intimate union between husband and wife. His *Theology of the Body* (TOB)[24] is the best source for guidance and developing awareness of what true marital love is supposed to look like. The basis for many of his talks on lust and infidelity revolve around Matthew 5:27-28, part of the

---

[23] Paul VI, *Humanae Vitae*, The Holy See, http://www.vatican.va/content/paul-vi/en/encyclicals/documents/hf_p-vi_enc_25071968_humanae-vitae.html, §13.

[24] John Paul II. *Man and Woman He Created Them: A Theology of the Body,* trans. Michael Waldstein (Boston, MA: Pauline Books & Media, 2006).

Sermon on the Mount where Jesus teaches, "You have heard that it was said, 'You shall not commit adultery.' But I say to you that every one who looks at a woman lustfully has already committed adultery with her in his heart." Saint John Paul II points out that in these words, Christ is saying that when a person looks at a woman lustfully he has stopped seeing the woman as a person, a beautiful child of God, and is objectifying her as if she's a mere possession and a piece of property (TOB 41:1). In these short verses, Jesus is referring to marital infidelity on a variety of levels, as we shall see. This "looking lustfully" can be the act of looking at other women with sexual desire in the heart, or looking at one's wife with the same intent—that of lust, not love.

> Adultery 'in the heart' is not committed only because the man 'looks' in this way at a woman who is not his wife but *precisely because he looks in this way at a woman. Even* if he were to look in this way at the woman who is his wife, he would commit the same adultery 'in the heart' (TOB 43:2).

That's why sexual coercion is subtle yet so traumatizing and psychologically cruel. When a man sexually coerces his wife to have sex with him, he's not thinking about her or her needs, nor is he considering his martial love for her. He's not seeking sexual intimacy for the purpose of mutual self-giving and reciprocal intimacy, for communion equal sharing, and he's not honoring the personal dignity of his "dearly beloved." Instead, he desires his own carnal gratification only. He doesn't care if his wife wants intimacy or not. *He* does, and his needs are paramount. After all, "men have needs," as he may have tried to convince you. He feels entitled, as if he somehow deserves it.

This is not love. This is lust, and it tells you his clear attitudes about intimacy and the marital act. If you're like so many who have endured this type of trauma, the message tears you apart; to him, sex is about the high, not about loving intimacy, mutual sharing of personhoods, respect, personal dignity, a complete giving of self. To him, sex is something else altogether. To him, sex is purely secular. This type of intimate trauma creates a deep internal scar that requires a great deal of spiritual healing to overcome. Betrayal trauma wounds us in the deepest, most interior parts of our core selves. When the one person we trusted the most to protect us, love us, and keep us safe instead harms us, the shock and impact is enormous.

St. John Paul II is very clear about this objectification of one's spouse and how it reflects man's sinfulness. Lust changes the very existence of a woman into a mere object "for" her husband, rather than a person sharing a life "with" her husband in a "communion of persons" (TOB 43:3). This is not only devastating to a marriage, but it can destroy the relationship at its very foundation. "Such a reduction has the effect that the person (in this case the woman) becomes for the other person (the man) above all an object for the possible satisfaction of his own sexual 'urge'" (TOB 43:3). This is a clear deformation of the naturally loving give-and-take nature of the marital bond.

St. John Paul II goes on to say:

The man who "looks" in the way described in Matthew 5:27-28 "makes use" of the woman, of her femininity, to satisfy his own "drive." Even if he does not use her in an external act, he has already taken such an attitude in his interior when he makes this decision about a particular woman. Adultery "in the heart" consists precisely in this (TOB 43:3).

When a man looks at any woman lustfully—and this includes not only in person but in photographs, websites, and pornography— he's objectifying that woman for his own sexual predatory needs and is being unfaithful in his marriage. "Adultery in the heart" is adultery. Christ makes that quite clear.

And it always leads to more.

The Gateway to Abuse: How Pornography Destroys Relationships

In today's world, pornography not only seems to be everywhere, but it's often viewed as "normal" and even "healthy." Whether it's soft porn in the form of sexy and objectifying ads for beer, trucks, clothing, movies, food, music—well, anything, really—to easily accessible hardcore porn on the internet, the over-sexualization of society has become a damaging wound. Is it inevitable that all guys— and, increasingly, women—interact with porn? Should we just shrug our shoulders and dismiss such behavior as "the way things are nowadays"?

No. Absolutely not. Pornography is destructive on so many levels. It isn't merely demeaning and vile, but it also contributes to the prevalence of domestic violence. Abuse expert Lundy Bancroft points out:

Most pornographic movies, magazines, and web sites can function as training manuals for abusers, whether they intend to or not, teaching that women are unworthy of respect and valuable only as sex objects for men. A great deal of mainstream pornographic material—not just the so-called "hard core"—contains stories and images showing the abuse of both women and children as sexy.[25]

It's time to recognize pornography for what it is—a gateway to abuse, an objectification of women, a dangerous addiction that demoralizes society and actually changes the structure of the brain.[26]

And it's a definite form of infidelity—a dishonoring of the sacred marriage vow and of the promise "to love and cherish, forsaking all others." The reasons why porn is so vile and dangerous are long and varied, so I'll focus on just a few.

First, instead of enjoying a sacred intimate bond with his wife—which entails not merely a physical aspect but a spiritual joining of two souls so "the two will become one flesh" (Gen. 2:24, Mark 10:8)—a man engaged in pornographic activity is enjoying a purely selfish fantasy of other women. He's engaging in lustful, isolated pleasure while disregarding the harm to self and others. He's enjoying images of other women, fantasizing of what he's doing to them

---

[25] Bancroft, *Why Does He Do That?, 327-328.*

[26] For more information, see the neurological studies and other information from Gary Wilson, "Brain Studies on Porn Users & Sex Addicts," Your Brain on Porn, https://www.yourbrainonporn.com/relevant-research-and-articles-about-the-studies/brain-studies-on-porn-users-sex-addicts/#brain.

or what they're doing to him. Even if he's not physically interacting with another woman, he's still getting perverse pleasure from her.

And that is cheating. Infidelity. Unfaithfulness.

There's no way around it: if your spouse is engaging in porn, he's cheating on you.

Most men who develop a porn addiction have done so out of hidden childhood wounds. Pornography is a "safe" means of escape from them—but, like any addiction, this isn't a healthy way to deal with trauma. If a man is authentically willing to change, to face those wounds head-on and not engage in addictive sexual behavior to soothe his anxiety, then there's hope. If he's not willing to face his inner demons, however, then the situation isn't likely to change.

It's also crucial to keep in mind that the porn industry obviously isn't a clean or healthy business to be in. Porn stars take a profusion of drugs or get drunk (usually both) just to get through the ordeal of filming, and many contract dangerous STDs.[27] To exploit someone else's pain through participation is abhorrent. There's also sex trafficking to consider. To support sex trafficking by engaging in porn is the utmost in human degradation.[28]

---

[27] Shelley Luben, "Ex-Porn Star Tells the Truth about the Porn Industry," Covenant Eyes, https://www.covenanteyes.com/2008/10/28/ex-porn-star-tells-the-truth-about-the-porn-industry/.

[28] Katherine Hamilton, "Here's How Your Porn Habit Could Be Helping Human Sex Traffickers," NBC News, https://nbc-2.com/news/2021/01/12/heres-how-your-porn-habit-could-be-helping-human-sex-traffickers/. See also Paul Bois, "Pornhub Under Fire After Videos of Rapes, Sex Trafficking Victims Posted to Site," The Daily Wire, https://www.dailywire.com/news/pornhub-under-fire-after-videos-of-rapes-sex-trafficking-victims-posted-to-site and Jonathan van Maren, "40

His pornography use becomes even more destructive when it enters your bedroom—and trust me, it eventually will, in one way or another.

One common side-effect of frequent porn use and masturbation is erectile dysfunction.[29] "If you are under 40, and not on specific medications, and don't have a serious medical or psychological condition, your copulatory ED almost certainly arises from performance anxiety or internet porn—or a combination of the two," be-set-selling author, speaking, and researcher Gary Wilson has pointed out.[30]

Another fact to consider is that pornography is full of sadistic and abusive images. Coercion, power-over, slaps, hits, bondage, verbal abuse, and other degrading actions are the norm. Most pornographic images and videos feed an abusive attitude and make such behaviors seem acceptable and even normal. Women are often portrayed as completely submissive to their male partners, doing whatever he wants, however he wants it—and she's often depicted as being turned on by being treated in nasty, crude, humiliating, and cruel ways.

Sex-Abuse Survivors Launch $40M Lawsuit Against Pornhub for Profiting from Illegal Vids," LifeSiteNews, https://www.lifesitenews.com/blogs/40-sex-abuse-survivors-launch-40m-lawsuit-against-pornhub-for-profiting-from-illegal-vids/.

[29] Chris McKenna, "Porn-Induced Erectile Dysfunction: The Science, Stats, and Stories of PIED," Covenant Eyes, https://www.covenanteyes.com/2017/08/07/porn-induced-ed-science-stats-stories-pied/.

[30] Gary Wilson, "Sexual Problems," Your Brain on Porn, https://www.yourbrainonporn.com/sexual-problems/.

It's common for porn-addled men to take this behavior into their bedroom and expect their wives to behave accordingly. When their partners don't live up to their lust-craved expectations they're accused of being cold, rigid or frigid, or old-fashioned and boring. Often, he'll wear his partner down or threaten her (with physical violence, emotional maltreatment, blame-inducing guilt, or the silent treatment) until she gives in out of exhaustion, fear, or a combination of both.

That, my dear readers, is not love, respect, devotion, or mutual self-giving.

That is sexual abuse. Plain and simple.

Individuals with an abuse problem are notorious for minimizing their behaviors—and pornography use is no exception. They excuse their actions by telling themselves—and you—that engaging in porn "doesn't mean anything" or "I was just watching." They say it's just "fantasy" and they were really thinking about you while masturbating to images of other women. "It's just entertainment" and "every man does it" are other common excuses. As award-winning author Chris Hedges says in his book *Empire of Illusion*, pornography "is about getting yourself off at someone else's expense."[31]

And that someone is you. And the actors demeaning themselves in such a way. And your children, because porn use naturally and always diminishes and degrades family life and interactions.

---

[31] Chris Hedges, *Empire of Illusion: The End of Literacy and the Triumph of Spectacle,* as quoted in Luke Gilkerson, "Yes, Porn is Cheating. Here's Why," Covenant Eyes, https://www.covenanteyes.com/2015/01/19/using-porn-is-cheating/.

Always remember, no matter what he may say or excuses he may make, his porn habit is a defilement of his role as spouse and father. It's infidelity. Unfaithfulness. A violation of your marriage in all ways imaginable: through lies, deceit, betraying a bond, abuse of self and you. It means he's leading a double life and is a chronic liar. And, like a mistress, it's something you don't need to tolerate.

The Catholic Church is clear regarding the sins of masturbation and pornography:

> Both the Magisterium of the Church and the moral sense of the faithful have been in no doubt and have firmly maintained that masturbation is an intrinsically and gravely disordered action. The deliberate use of the sexual faculty, for whatever reason, outside of marriage is essentially contrary to its purpose. For here sexual pleasure is sought outside of the sexual relationship which is demanded by the moral order and in which the total meaning of mutual self-giving and human procreation in the context of true love is achieved (CCC 2352).

> It offends against chastity because it perverts the conjugal act, the intimate giving of spouses to each other. It does grave injury to the dignity of its participants (actors, vendors, the public), since each one becomes an object of base pleasure and illicit profit for others ... It is a grave offense (CCC 2354).

In today's world, these teachings cannot be repeated enough. Sexuality is taken for granted, and infidelity is only acknowledged if there's been physical cheating. Marital infidelity in all its forms— and even worse, marital sexual assault—is barely (if ever) recognized by the secular culture at large. It's time to set the record straight and re-read Jesus' Sermon on the Mount in light of St. John Paul II's teaching on the *Theology of the Body*. Since God doesn't lie, we should take Him seriously.

Chapter Six

The Most Abused Verses in the Bible

"Wives, be subject to your husbands, as to the Lord."

(Eph. 5:22)

Abuse makes us feel weak. Most likely we've been criticized, belittled, subjugated, controlled by fear and threats, called names, made to feel as if we're crazy—or all the above. Being forced to associate with an abusive person causes damage and has a tremendous impact on all areas of life. Effects of abuse often include:

- Psychological (such as fear of losing one's memory, of going crazy, falling into clinical depression, confusion, being in a constant fog, anxiety, panic attacks, fear)
- Physical (including migraines, stomach issues, heart conditions, menstruation problems, sleep disturbances, chronic pain)
- Emotional and spiritual (despair, losing hope, anguish, loss of trust in self and in humanity in general)
- And more. So much more.

When we feel weak, one of the best healing resources available to us is that of Sacred Scripture. There are so many inspirational and supportive verses in the Bible that it's impossible to quote them all, but here's a brief sampling:

- "God is our refuge and strength, a very present help in trouble. Therefore we will not fear though the earth should change, though the mountains shake in the heart of the sea … *Be still and know that I Am God*" (Ps. 46:1-2,10).

- "Strength and honour are her clothing; she shall rejoice at the time to come" (Prov. 31:25).

- "But now thus says the LORD, He who created you … 'Fear not, for I have redeemed you; I have called you by name, you are Mine. When you pass through the waters I will be with you; and through the rivers, they shall not overwhelm you; when you walk through the fire you shall not be burned, and the flame shall not consume you … Because you are precious in My eyes, and honored, and I love you … Fear not, for I am with you'" (Isa. 43:1-2,4-5).

- "God is faithful, and He will not let you be tempted beyond your strength, but with the temptation will also provide the way of escape, that you may be able to endure it" (1 Cor. 10:13).

- "We are afflicted in every way, but not crushed; perplexed, but not driven to despair; persecuted, but not forsaken; struck down, but not destroyed." (2 Cor. 4:8-9).

However, there are some biblical verses that may seem hurtful and even retraumatizing when taken out of context, especially when manipulative people claim certain passages of Sacred Scripture support their twisted viewpoints. The USCCB states:

As bishops, we condemn the use of the Bible to support abusive behavior in any form. A correct reading of Scripture leads people to an understanding of the equal dignity of men and women and to relationships based on mutuality and love.[32]

"Wives must be submissive to their husbands"

It's time to dive into the most notorious Bible verse in the history of … well, Bible verses. It's the line women dread and controlling men love to take out of context and interpret according to their own whims and wishes. Yes, you guessed it: the widely-misinterpreted text of Ephesians 5:22. "Wives, be subject to your husbands, as to the Lord."

What are we to make of that, as we peer through our modern-colored glasses and gasp in alarm? St. Paul was a misogynist, obviously. What a jerk.

But wait. One step at a time. First, it's crucial not to read this verse in isolation, as is so often done. If we see the big picture, the entire vision as St. Paul intended rather than picking and choosing words as if we're at a buffet, something miraculous happens: rather than a message of misogynistic condemnation, the verse actually elevates women and speaks of love and mutual self-giving. As historian and biblical scholar Carl. J. Sommer points out, in writing

---

[32] USCCB, "When I Call for Help."

Ephesians St. Paul proved himself to be "a social innovator of great daring."[33]

History Lesson 101: The Greco-Roman World in the First Century A.D.

Although Ephesians 5:22—"Wives, be subject [or submissive] to your husbands"—is one of the favored Bible quotes of abusive men who try to use spirituality as a weapon against their targets, what's not usually mentioned or even known is that the word "submissive" (υποτασσομαι) isn't even in the original Greek text. The literal translation of Ephesians 5:22 from Greek to English is "The wives to their own husbands as to the Lord." We have to go back to Ephesians 5:21 to find the Greek word for "submissive," and this verse refers to mutual submission of husband and wife, not a power-over type of submission that infers coercive control and absolute, monarch-like rule.

Paul uses the word "submissive" in the verses both before and after 5:22 to reinforce his insistence upon complementarity within marriage. Respect and love are foundations of a marital union, taking the form of mutual self-giving which both husband and wife must be in submission to—in other words, mutual cooperation, kindness, communication, and authentic love. When read properly—particularly keeping the historical context in mind—what we discover in the book of Ephesians is a beautiful theology of mutual submission to marital love, fidelity, respect, and union.

---

[33] Carl J. Sommer, *We Look For a Kingdom: The Everyday Lives of the Early Christians* (San Francisco, CA: Ignatius Press, 2007), 298.

Considering the Greek and Roman cultural norms of the day, St. Paul's teaching becomes even more astounding. The idea of mutual submission was completely unknown in the Greco-Roman world of St. Paul, which shows how radical the newly-forming Christian theology truly was. Beginning in the fourth-century B.C. with Aristotle, "household codes" were used to instruct men on how to properly rule their homes—and wives were considered a mere step above servants. Paul takes this traditional formula as a basis for Ephesians 5, but adapts it in such a way that "he significantly qualifies its meaning, earning himself a place among the most progressive of ancient writers."[34] Craig S. Keener, professor of Biblical Studies at Asbury Seminary, also notes:

> Nearly every ancient Mediterranean society expected wives to submit to their husbands ... Household codes instructed male heads of households how to rule wives, children and slaves; while continuing to uphold the call for subordinates to submit, Paul here goes beyond traditional expectations in calling for *mutual* submission (cf. general Christian servanthood to one another in Mark 10:42-45; John 13:14-15; Gal. 5:13). This places Paul among the small proportion of ancient thinkers who valued mutual concern and sensitivity ...

---

[34] Craig S. Keener, *Paul, Women & Wives: Marriage and Women's Ministry in the Letters of Paul* (Peabody, MA: Hendrickson Publishers, Inc., 1992), 134.

It should go without saying that this is a general principle not applicable to situations of abuse or participation of sin.[35]

Roman society was shifting in St. Paul's day, and slowly women were gaining more power. This was a huge threat to the aristocratic male Romans, who balked at giving away any of their control. Of particular concern was the strange cult of the followers of Jesus of Nazareth, who seemed to place more importance and equality on women than the Roman patriarchal society felt was proper or safe.[36]

St. Paul knew he had to find a balance between respecting the culture of the day while at the same time reforming it to the Christ-centered ideal of mutual self-giving and authentic charity. He knew if he spoke too boldly, he'd create an uproar that would spark severe Christian persecution. At the same time, he had to preach God's truth about the mutuality of men and women. He did this in Ephesians 5, creating a balance between the standard ideals of the day and the generous Christian outlook that all people—Jew and Greek, male and female, slave and free—are created in the image and likeness of God, and all are equally redeemed by Christ (Gal 3:28).

St. Paul "calls on husbands to love their wives in such a radical way that husbands become their wives' servants, too."[37]

---

[35] Craig S. Keener, "Marriage Roles in Antiquity," in *NIV Cultural Backgrounds Study Bible: Bringing to Life the Ancient World of Scripture*, ed. Craig S. Keener and John H. Walton (Grand Rapids, MI: Zondervan, 2016), 2064 and 2066.

[36] Keener, *Paul, Women & Wives*, 139-145.

[37] Keener, *Paul, Women & Wives*, 166.

Mutual Self-Giving in Marriage

Interpreting Ephesians 5:22 as "wives must be submissive to their husbands" and then using this to "prove" the subordination of women is to abuse God's word. Denial of its true meaning, twisting its intent, using the words as a means of gaslighting to convince others that the true meaning is inaccurate, are all ways of desecrating the Holy Bible.

As St. Pope John Paul II stated, Ephesians 5:21

> expresses a different concept instead, namely that it is in her relationship with Christ—who is for both spouses the one and only Lord—that the wife can and should find the motivation for the relationship with her husband ... This relationship is nevertheless not one-sided submission (TOB 89:3).

Although Ephesians offers a revolutionary worldview on marital equality and mutual submission in the love of Christ, we often miss St. Paul's meaning because we're so inclined to interpret Scripture through a modern viewpoint. *We must avoid this temptation at all costs.* To read the Bible as if it should be a contemporary commentary on life and cultural norms is not only to miss the full richness contained in all the books, but it's also a dangerous way of misreading and thereby misunderstanding God's holy word.

Authentic Submission, the Opposite of Abuse

An additional—and crucial—concept in St. Paul's teaching on mutual submission within marriage is his comparison of the marital bond to the bond between Christ and His Church. Since Christ "gave Himself up for [the Church]" (Eph. 5:25), and Paul gives a comparison of husband/Christ, wife/Church, this means a husband is to wholly give himself to his wife in the same way Christ gave Himself to the Church—which, by the sheer nature of love and self-giving, means abuse is not an option.

We should willingly give our submission to Christ because we can trust Him with all our hearts, all our souls, all our minds, and all our strength (Mark 12:30). He wants the best for us, always and everywhere, without exception. He won't abuse or misuse our love, but will rather transform it into something even deeper, richer, bolder—mere water into the choicest wine.

We should submit to God because that's the only true way to live.

This, amazingly, is what St. Paul is telling spouses they must do in order to live a rich, full, authentic marital life together. Husband and wife must be mutually submissive, in Christ. They must fully and unreservedly give of their whole selves. They must, without hesitation, gift their spouse with the beauty of their vulnerability.

This can only be done through trust and reciprocated love. "Love is patient, love is kind; love is not jealous or boastful; it is not arrogant or rude. Love does not insist on its own way; it is not irritable or resentful" (1 Cor. 13:4–5).

If you're experiencing "love" that's jealous, boastful, arrogant, rude, insisting on its own way, irritable or resentful, you're not experiencing authentic, Christ-driven love. It's risky to expose your vulnerable self-giving within the context of such a relationship, because self-giving must be mutual.

God always wants the best for you; He knows what you need even before you do; He will never abuse your love but will nurture and treasure it. If you're to love your spouse in Christ and be willing to submit yourself to your spouse, in Christ, you have to be assured you can do so in the same way and with the same trust as you submit to God. If not—if you can't trust, if your partner consistently neglects your good in preference to his own needs, if he lacks the awareness to even recognize your needs, hurts, and faithfulness—then submitting your love could be detrimental to your psychological, emotional, spiritual, and physical wellbeing.

Ephesians 5:21-33 simply cannot apply to abusive relationships. How can it, when one spouse refuses to love in Christ? Since St. Paul is writing about mutual self-giving ("be subject to one another"), submission can't be one-sided. If a man doesn't "love his wife as himself," how can the wife fully trust her husband? Quite simply, she can't—nor should she. Otherwise, she'll put herself at an even greater risk. She has already been betrayed.

The question is, will her spouse be a repentant Peter, who after his betrayal of Christ affirmed his love three times in authentic humility, or will he be a Judas, who simply gave up and didn't even try to repent, make amends, or change?

Theology of the Body

St. Pope John Paul II wrote extensively about the beauty of Christ-centered marriage, particularly in *Theology of the Body*:

> [St. Paul in the book of Ephesians] writes, "And you, husbands, love your wives," and with this way of expressing himself he takes away any fear that could have been created (given contemporary sensibility) by the earlier sentence, "Wives, be subject to your husbands." Love excludes every kind of submission by which the wife would become a servant or slave of the husband, an object of one-sided submission ... The community or unity that they should constitute because of marriage is realized through a reciprocal gift, which is also a mutual submission (TOB 89:4).

In his apostolic letter *Mulieus Dignitatem* (*On the Dignity and Vocation of Women*), St. Pope John Paul II wrote, "The matrimonial union requires respect for and a perfecting of the true personal subjectivity of both of them. *The woman cannot become the 'object' of 'domination' and male 'possession.'*"[38]

As we can see in the writing of St. Paul, this attitude of mutual loving within a marital bond has been a part of Catholic teaching since the beginning and has been crucial throughout our faith history. The early Church Father John Chrysostom, who lived in the

---

[38] St. Pope John Paul II, *Mulieus Dignitatem*, The Holy See, https://www.vatican.va/content/john-paul-ii/en/apost_letters/1988/ documents/hf_jp-ii_apl_19880815_mulieris-dignitatem.html, 10.

fourth century, spoke extensively on the book of Ephesians. In his homily on Ephesians 5 he said:

> The partner of one's life, the mother of one's children, the foundation of one's every joy, one ought never to chain down by fear and menaces, but with love and good temper. For what sort of union is that, where the wife trembles at her husband? And what sort of pleasure will the husband himself enjoy, if he dwells with his wife as with a slave, and not as with a free-woman? [39]

A wife cannot be subject to her husband as to the Lord if there is fear and domination in the relationship, because in the Lord there is no fear, but only peace; there is no domination, only love (John 14:27, 2 Tim. 1:7, 1 John 4:18).

God endowed us with the gift of free will because He wants our love. He doesn't coerce us by fear. God doesn't want to control us, but He does want us to control ourselves. This is the model for all our relationships.

If He Hits You, Should You Encourage Him to Hit You Again?

Another abused Bible passage that can't be overlooked is Matthew 5:38-39 (also Luke 6:29): "'You have heard that it was said, "An eye for an eye and a tooth for a tooth." But I say to you, do not resist

---

[39] St. John Chrysostom, "*Homily on Ephesians:* Homily 20," New Advent, https://www.newadvent.org/fathers/230120.htm

one who is evil. But if any one strikes you on the right cheek, turn to him the other also.'"

Does this mean Jesus wants us to simply curl up in a ball and accept mistreatment?

Hardly. This verse isn't about domestic violence, and to interpret it in such a way is another misreading of Sacred Scripture. What this verse does teach us is how to engage in non-violent yet firm resistance. Jesus isn't inviting us to accept unjust mistreatment, nor is he encouraging us to allow others to beat us or violate our spirits, minds, or bodies. As always, reading Sacred Scripture in historical context is critical.

In verse 38, Jesus refers to the Mosaic civil law (eye for eye, tooth for tooth ...", Ex. 21:24), which was put in place as a way of restricting unjust revenge against others. Mosaic law made it clear that the punishment needed to fit the crime and should never be inappropriately extreme.

By citing Mosaic law and taking it one step further, Jesus is in no way advocating the uncharitable, unmerciful, and unjust violation of domestic abuse, nor is he telling victims to "shut up and put up." Rather, Jesus is making it clear that when we're abused, we're not to retaliate by becoming an abuser ourselves.

If your husband hits you, don't hit him back; if he shouts at you and calls you nasty names, don't seek revenge by doing the same.

Rather than revenge, Jesus tells us to "pray for those who persecute you" (Matt. 5:44), yet this doesn't mean we have to actively engage with abuse or even remain in a toxic situation. When Saul attacked David and tried to pin him to the wall with a spear, David didn't accept the assault without resistance. Instead, "David fled and escaped that night" (1 Sam. 19:10). Jesus himself escaped his attackers when they sought to kill him, rather than sticking around to accept unjust abuse (Luke 4:29-30, John 8:59, 10:39).

The verses that follow Matthew 5:39 are also insightful, even if they don't seem to be at first glance. Jesus tells his listeners, "if any one would sue you and take your coat, let him have your cloak as well; and if any one forces you to go a mile, go with him two miles" (Matt. 5:40-41). When read with a modern mindset, this certainly appears as if Jesus is telling us to accept mistreatment at the hands of others without any objection, and in fact to encourage more.

Yet that's not at all what he's saying.

In Jesus' day people wore two garments, an inner and an outer. If they were sued in court, they could be sued for their outer garment, but not the inner one. It was the inner garment that protected them from the cold and prevented them from being naked. Being naked in public was against Roman law—it was even illegal to look at a naked person. Jesus' original audience would immediately have recognized the irony of his statement. If a person gave his inner garment as well as his outer, the Roman soldiers and even the judges would be forced to arrest themselves for violating their own law by looking upon a naked person.

As for walking a mile, Roman soldiers often forced underprivileged Jews to carry their heavy packs for them, a right they extended to Jesus at his crucifixion when they forced Simon of Cyrene to carry the cross. However, by law they could only force someone to walk one mile—anything further than that was a violation of Roman law. Therefore, if a person was ordered by a soldier to walk a mile, yet that person walked two instead, the Roman solider would be the one in violation of the law.[40]

These ironies show the heart and delightful beauty of Jesus' teaching on nonviolent resistance. As renowned biblical scholars Raymond Brown, Joseph Fitzmyer, and Roland Murphy point out, "Jesus' teaching is a strategy for winning, not for passive resignation or indifference to evil. The goal is to shame the opponent into a change of heart."[41]

Love Your Enemies …

What about "Love your neighbor as yourself" (Mark 12:31, also Luke 6:27 and Matt. 5:44-45)? Doesn't this indicate an obligation to stay with an abusive partner, as so many claim?

Not at all.

First, this verse shows us that we also must respect—and cherish—ourselves, recognizing that we're all "made in the image and likeness" of God—and God doesn't want Him image abused (Gen. 1:26).

We can love others, while at the same time not tolerate their mistreatment and manipulations. To claim "love your neighbors" or "love your enemies" means we should allow ourselves to be

---

[40] Amy-Jill Levine and Marc Zvi Brettler, eds., *The Jewish Annotated New Testament: Second Edition*, NRSV (NY: Oxford University Press, 2011), 21.

[41] Raymond E. Brown, Joseph A. Fitzmyer, and Roland E. Murphy, eds, *The New Jerome Biblical Commentary* (Englewood Cliffs, NJ: Prentice Hall, Inc., 1990), 644.

mistreated and to stay in an emotionally, physically, or psychologically dangerous marriage is the same as claiming the slaves in pre-Civil War days should have put up with their lot in life, and that it was wrong for anyone to fight for their emancipation.

I think we can all agree that's twisted thinking.

"Love from a distance" is often the safest—and only—course in relationships where an abuser refuses to change. St. Paul, in his first letter to the Corinthians, stated: "I wrote to you not to associate with any one who bears the name of brother if he is guilty of immorality or greed, or is an idolater, reviler, drunkard, or robber—not even to eat with such a one" (1 Cor. 5:11).

Yes, love those who mistreat you because they're children of God—but there's no biblical or moral obligation to love them as lovers if they adamantly refuse to see the error of their ways. "As for a man who is factious, after admonishing him once or twice, have nothing to do with him, knowing that such a person is perverted and sinful; he is self-condemned" (Titus 3:10).

Take Up Your Cross. Jesus Says So!

It's true, Christ has told us all that we'll all endure suffering in this fallen world, and that "taking up our cross" and shouldering the burden of our suffering results in immeasurable graces. Yet what does this truly mean?

Another misread and abused verse in the Bible is again from the Gospel of Matthew, this time in chapter sixteen. "Then Jesus said to his disciples, 'Whoever wishes to come after me must deny himself, take up his cross, and follow me'" (Matt. 16:24, also Lk. 9:23). This verse has been cited by not only abusers, but also well-meaning yet extremely under-informed clergy, Christian therapists, and other lay ministers as a reason why women in abusive marriages should tolerate their situation.

However, "taking up one's cross" does not mean laying down like a beaten dog and accepting more violence, more mistreatment, more decimation of one's spirit, one's psyche, one's God-given life.

Quite the opposite, in fact.

St. John Paul II, in his message at the 16th annual World Youth Day on February 14, 2001, eloquently described what it truly means to "take up one's cross":

> *Take up his cross daily and follow me."* As the cross can be reduced to being an ornament, "to carry the cross" can become just a manner of speaking. In the teaching of Jesus, however, it does not imply the pre-eminence of mortification and denial. It does not refer primarily to the need to endure patiently the great and small tribulations of life, or, even less, to the exaltation of pain as a means of pleasing God. It is not suffering for its own sake that a Christian seeks, but love. When the cross is embraced it becomes a sign of love and of total self-giving. To carry it behind Christ means to be united with him in offering the greatest proof of love. We cannot speak about the cross without considering God's love

for us, the fact that God wishes to shower us with good things.[42]

The cross is about love, not control and abuse. It isn't about "the need to endure patiently" or the obligation to silently put up with toxic treatment. "Do you not know that your body is a temple of the Holy Spirit within you, which you have from God?" (1 Cor. 6:19)

In abusive marriages where the offending partner refuses to authentically and permanently give up control and change his ways, the cross the victim carries is that of coming to terms with the fact that her marriage isn't safe, holy, or healthy. Taking firm action against mistreatment is a cross in itself.

In the same World Youth Day message, St. John Paul II also stated that "to deny oneself is to give up one's own plans in order to accept God's plan." In other words, to accept God's will for our lives—no matter what that will may be. Sometimes "denying oneself and taking up one's cross" means giving up plans for a "happily ever after" future and coming to the shocking realization and acceptance that separation, and perhaps even divorce, may be God's will. Each situation is different, and every marriage is unique, but in all relationships one truth remains the same—*there is no excuse for abuse.* And no one should be forced to endure it.

---

[42] St. John Paul II, "Message of the Holy Father to the Youth of the World on the Occasion of the XVI World Youth Day," the Holy See, https://www.vatican.va/content/john-paul-ii/en/messages/youth/documents/hf_jp-ii_mes_20010215_xvi-world-youth-day.html

The Forgiveness Deception

In Matthew 18:21-22 we read: "Then Peter came up and said to him, 'Lord, how often shall my brother sin against me, and I forgive him? As many as seven times?' Jesus said to him, 'I do not say to you seven times, but seventy times seven.'"

An abuser who professes to be a Christian may claim, "See, Jesus said you have to forgive me, no matter how many times I mess up"— and he'll use that as an excuse to continue his toxic behaviors. He'll also expect you to forget what he's done, to erase it from your memory as if he'd never harmed you—not caring or even considering the damage that does to your emotional, psychological, and spiritual well-being.

It's interesting to notice that immediately after Jesus spoke about forgiving "not seven times, but seventy times seven," he then launched into what we now call "the parable of the unmerciful servant" (Matt. 18:23-35). This unmerciful servant was the guy whose financial debt was forgiven by his king—but then he turned around and demanded repayment for a lesser debt that was owed him by another. When the king found out, he was justifiably enraged.

What's so intriguing about this parable is how the story describes what forgiveness is—and what it isn't.

Here are the key points we need to notice. First, the king forgives the high debt of his servant—which corresponds to Jesus' teaching about forgiving others "seventy times seven." However, the servant himself refuses to forgive the lesser debt of another, which proves this servant to be ungrateful, unrepentant, and unchanging in his selfish toxic behaviors. Mercy given to him didn't cause him to gain empathy or become merciful to another. He didn't learn from his mistakes nor gain virtue or insight from the forgiveness given to him; instead, he took that forgiveness and abused it by steadfastly refusing mercy to another.

What happens next? Does the king "forgive and forget" this latest transgression of his servant?

No.

Instead, the king throws the servant into jail until the time when he's willing to pay all his debt.

What does this tell us about the nature of forgiveness, particularly when Jesus' words about forgiving "seventy times seven" are used as an excuse for continuing abusive behavior?

Jesus makes it clear through the parable of the unmerciful servant that a remorseless sinner earns his just fruits. Repentance must be honest—otherwise it's not true repentance, it's just another churn of the abuse cycle.

Even when repentance is authentic, automatic, and forced forgiveness isn't something a survivor is obligated to do, at least not at first. I realize this may sound as if it's in opposition to Jesus' teaching in Matthew 18:21-22, and that's why I've dedicated an entire section of chapter ten to "the art of forgiveness."

Those who expect Christ-like mercy must be merciful to others. They must feel genuine remorse and be repentant for what they've done, but repentance isn't a matter of stained-glass words and perhaps a bouquet of roses. Abusers often apologize for their behavior immediately after an abusive incident, but that apology is only authentic if it's not used as a "get out of jail free" card—in other words, an excuse to encourage you to "forgive and forget" and move on, while the abusive cycle continues to revolve week after week, month after month, year after year. True remorse must be genuine, an interior stirring of the heart (Ps. 51:10), followed by authentic and permanent change (including professional and spiritual help). Otherwise, it's nothing but fog, visible one moment and dissipated the next.

Continued abuse is the opposite of mercy and repentance.

Besides, forced "forgiveness" in the form of ignoring toxic behavior, without holding the guilty party responsible for their words, attitudes, and actions, is actually enabling them to sin, which is the opposite of Christ's teachings. Going back further in the same chapter of Matthew, Jesus tells us, "If your brother sins against you, go and tell him his fault, between you and him alone. If he listens to you, you have gained your brother ... If he refuses to listen ... let him be to you as a Gentile and a tax collector" (Matt. 18:15,17). Jesus is clearly saying that forgiveness doesn't equal reconciliation, nor does it mean ignoring the transgression and pretending it didn't happen.

But, again, more on that later.

I'm closing this chapter with a quote of inspiration: "Do not throw away your confidence, which has great reward. For you have need of endurance, so that you may do the will of God and receive what is promised" (Heb. 10:35-36).

How can we discern the will of God, and what is the promise we're to receive? The answer is simple: as children of God, we're called to thrive in His grace, sheltered under His comforting wings (Psalm 17:8, 36:7, 61:4, 91:4), to draw ever closer to Him. Often, we focus more on our tumultuous relationship than on Him. Spiritual drought can be a result of abuse; we tend to neglect our spiritual lives because all our focus is on the daily crazy-making and other abusive patterns we've been forced to endure. When we shift gears, when we take time for self-care by opening ourselves more to God through prayer, daily devotions such as the rosary and the Liturgy of the Hours, and inspirational spiritual reading (particularly Sacred Scripture), we find greater peace and more stability of mind. This stability of mind then helps us, through the guidance of the Holy Spirit, to make the decisions we need to make based on His will for our lives.

And the promise? The peace of God will abound, no matter what decisions need to be made. "Peace I leave with you; my peace I give to you" (John 14:27).

Chapter Seven

Discerning God's Will for Your Life

"For everything there is a season ...
a time to embrace, and a time to refrain from embracing."

(Eccles. 3:1,5)

Should you stay in your relationship, or would it be best to finally leave? Only you can answer that question. We've all been given the gift of free will, so we must make our own choices. Yet at the same time, we've also been graced with the intuition of the Holy Spirit, that "still, small voice" (1 Kings 19:12) speaking to us out of the depths of our soul, guiding and advising. The problem is, we often don't want to listen to that Voice, because God's will for us seems to be in opposition to our personal will for ourselves—either that or we simply fail to hear because our trauma is too distracting, a "noisy gong, or a clanging cymbal" within our battered and confused souls (1 Cor. 13:1).

Yet we have to listen and listen closely. "He who has ears to hear, let him hear" (Matt. 11:15). Even when we don't want to accept God's answer, we must listen with open ears, and an open mind.

As I mentioned earlier, if you're in physical danger, please seek help immediately. The appendix at the back of this book will give you some resources. And of course, pray always. Trust God. "Do not fear" (Matt. 10:28). Yet at the same time, be wise and alert, "be sober, be watchful." (1 Pet. 5:8). Take every precaution to protect yourself and your children.

Before I go further, I want to reassure you that the Catholic Church doesn't expect anyone in an abusive marriage to remain stuck in such a toxic environment. I write more about the Church's stance on this issue in the next chapter.

An Abusive Marriage is a Lonely Marriage

Nothing is lonelier than feeling alone in a marriage, yet this kind of aching emptiness is one of the consequences of domestic abuse.

Loneliness is all-encompassing, creeping from your heart to your soul and enveloping everything in between. It can often be felt deep within the body in a physical way, as a heaviness in the chest or an ache in the gut. It reaches to all parts of a person and leaves us bereft, restless, and joyless. Loneliness is soul-wrenching, because God made us social creatures designed to share our lives and loves, hurts and sorrows. This is an inherent part of humanity—after all, even Adam, living in the glory of paradise, cried out to God to give him a companion of the soul.

Even worse than the ache of general loneliness is being lonely when not physically alone. By its very nature, an abusively toxic relationship doesn't allow for true tenderness, mutual self-giving, or "the intimate community of life and love which constitutes the married state" (CCC 1603). The CCC further says that marriage "is by its nature ordered toward the good of the spouses" (CCC 1601), yet when one spouse emotionally, physically, psychologically, or verbally batters the other, that spouse is certainly not concerned with the good of his partner. He's focused only on what he perceives to be the good of himself.

Such toxic treatment results in emotional stagnation and alienation. If you have to walk on eggshells within your own home—creeping around the house in order to avoid another incident, cautious of your every word and action to be sure you're dodging anything that might set off an explosion of abusive anger or covert control—then getting close on an emotional level is likely the last thing on your mind. It often feels too dangerous, and in fact it *is* to vulnerable and dangerous. It would be like getting too close to a striking cobra. Why would anyone want to do that? Yet the pain of being in this situation is excruciating. As St. Teresa of Calcutta said, "The most terrible poverty is loneliness, and the feeling of being unloved."

Marital loneliness is one of the worst kinds of anguish. To be bereft of love, friendship, and companionship while involved in an intimate relationship is bewildering and crazy-making, to say the least. On top of it all, self-blame is a huge and corrosive issue within lonely marriages. It's difficult to make sense of why Prince Charming so often turns into the Big Bad Wolf, ready to do anything to ensnare his target. When you're repeatedly told you're the problem and you're to blame, you likely tend to accept the accusations as truth because you naturally love and trust the person who has promised to love and trust you. What you need to realize is that if he's abusive, nothing he says can be trusted—because he's not to be trusted as long as he continues with his toxic behaviors.

Yet all this—the self-blame, the confusion as to why he claims he's not at fault, the criticisms mixed with the times of loving compliments and seeming support, the lack of emotional availability, his voice claiming "I love you" while his actions say "I really think you're a piece of crap" (and sometimes being told that outright), the controlling possessiveness and jealousy, the unfair and unjust accusations of wrongdoing, negative intent, and possible infidelity … all of this swirls within your mind until you're left with a searing hollowness that's difficult to define.

The reason this feeling is so confusing is because if you're still enmeshed in a toxic relationship, you may not recognize your anguish as loneliness. After all, you're not physically alone.

Yet emotionally, you're stranded on a deserted island. This emotional loneliness is deeper than physical loneliness because it's so wrong and counterintuitive. You shouldn't have to be lonely in a marriage. The very idea is topsy-turvy. The truth is, whether you consciously realize it or not, chances are you're in mourning. You shouldn't be lonely because you have a partner, yet you're even lonelier than you would be if you were single.

You're mourning an illusion, something you likely never had even though it was promised in a sacred vow. This anguish is also deeply spiritual in nature. To be solitary, to be unable to turn to the one person who is supposed provide unconditional friendship and love—yet to have him standing right there, physically present—often feels unbearable.

It's important to recognize this piercing hollowness for what it truly is. Only in the recognition can you begin to heal this wound and to find the love, trust and support you so achingly need.

Yet where can this love be found?

You have to enter into your loneliness, not wish it away or seek to avoid it. As strange as it sounds, embrace the loneliness. Live it, and live within it. It's only when you allow the space to go within and develop a relationship with your innermost self that you can then find the strength to transform your loneliness into restorative stillness.

This quiet stillness is the treasure of authentic interior peace. Cultivating this inner peace will allow you to thrive despite outward turmoil. And, it's in finding this soul space that you'll finally be able to grasp—and gain strength from—an intrinsic beauty and fortitude that will not tolerate abuse, in any form, ever again. It's then that you can learn the true meaning of Jesus' words when he said, "Love your neighbor as yourself" (Mark 12:31). Loving neighbor as self presupposes that you truly love yourself. When you love yourself in a pure, authentic way, loneliness becomes stillness of the heart; anguish becomes harmony within the soul.

It seems so easy to read about this inner peace, yet so difficult to actually cultivate it. The concept can seem amorphous, vague, lovely in writing but impossible in doing. Indeed, it is difficult to grasp, and not something you can force or coerce.

That's why asking for help is critical.

No one can make this transformation alone. As fallible human beings, none of us are capable of that, because we're all dependent upon God's grace. We need the guidance of the Spirit, the One Who Is, to help fill us. Betrayal and abuse breaks us open, causing us to acutely feel the raw interior of loneliness. God fills this raw interior with His flowing graces—if we allow our sore selves to remain open enough to receive those graces. Yes, suffering hurts. A lot. But through the pain, there is relief. Relief, release, and resurrection.

Once you fill yourself with the peace of the Holy Spirit, the rest will begin to fall into place. This is because you're allowing it—you're opening yourself to the fullness of grace, to the exploration of understanding your deep inner worth and reexamining your true self. Yes, you still need human camaraderie, healthy relationships, and authentic friends. Yet when you release the toxins created by abuse and manipulation, and fill that space with genuine love of self, the ache of loneliness transforms into the joy of life.

The path of healing is the path of prayer. Talk to God, and He will talk to you.

Understanding Your Intuition

We all have a knowledge deep within us, an intuitive understanding and discernment. This voice within is divine guidance, which quite often is very difficult to hear. It's the voice that tells us— *Stop! Don't go there!* or *All is well, proceed with joy.* Yet there are so many obstacles in life that drown out our confidence to trust our reality and intuition.

Some people call this knowingness their gut instinct, others prefer to think of it as their intuition. As Christians, we're able to recognize our inner knowingness as that "still small Voice" of the Holy Spirit, forever urging, guiding, and protecting us (1 Kings 19:12).

The problem with such a soft voice is that it's often drowned out by the rumble and rubble of outer voices, particularly in the case of spousal abuse. Abuse causes confusion, clouded reasoning, distorted judgment, "abuse amnesia" (when a victim suppresses the memory of distressing incidents so as to not experience greater levels of distress), and other negative psychological consequences. The effects of such enormous trauma are far-reaching and pervasive, all-encompassing, and consuming.

Domestic abuse has likely stifled your ability to hear—and trust—the "small still Voice" within. Your sense of self may feel shredded as you struggle to get through each day. Abuse causes a loss of self-trust as, through the tactics of gaslighting and crazy-making, you're slowly brainwashed into doubting your own perceptions of reality and intuitive beliefs. Many people have described the experience of being in an abusive relationship as "walking on eggshells" because it's so difficult to discern up from down, right from left, back from forth.

Chances are you never know who will walk through the door at the end of the workday. Will it be Dr. Jekyll, or Mr. Hyde? If it's a good day and Dr. Jekyll shows up, how long will he stay before Hyde saunters in to take his place? You may find yourself constantly monitoring what you say, how your facial expressions are arranged, and every other aspect of your entire beinghood, all in an effort not to trigger the metamorphosis from Jekyll to Hyde.

This isn't walking on eggshells—it's walking on glass. It may hurt a bit if you walk barefoot on crumbly eggshells, but the pain will be minimal. If you walk barefoot over glass, however, your skin will be slashed to shreds and the glass will imbed itself inside your flesh. This glass will be difficult and painful to remove, but it's possible—yet healing can only occur after all the wounding pieces are completely gone from deep inside your skin.

This abuse is precisely why your intuition, once so keen and sharp, seems to have disappeared. But it hasn't. Your intuition remains as that "still small Voice" of knowingness. Your abuser's voice is rowdy, obnoxious, hurtful, accusatory, derogatory, and deeply devastating. It sounds louder than the still small Voice within. It can drown out that Voice, but it can never obliterate it.

Slow down. Breathe. Listen. And stop listening.

It's essential to stop listening to the voice of your abuser and start listening to the Voice of the Spirit, internally guiding you. Calm your nervous system through prayer, deep breathing, and reaching out for help. Connect with supporting and informed loved ones, a trusted spiritual resource, or professional help. Be not afraid. Self-love and self-care will begin the process of regaining self-trust.

Quite often your intuition will tell you the opposite of what your abuser claims. Perhaps subtle traces of porn were discovered on his computer, which he vehemently denies and explains with a variety of nearly-plausible excuses, yet that Voice tugging from within keeps whispering that he's lying. Or maybe it's a more vague, yet quite insistent, sense that your partner isn't being honest about something—or many things. There's a feeling of definite knowingness—somehow, you just *know* that something isn't quite right, even if what that *something* is can't be defined.

It's easy to wonder if such a subtle feeling should be ignored, especially when the lies and gaslighting are at a confusing peak.

As you break free from the toxins of abuse, you'll find yourself becoming more and more able to hear the Voice of the Holy Spirit within. By developing or maintaining a deep prayer life, asking the Lord for His wisdom, discernment, and guidance, you can open your heart and mind to His healing graces. Praying daily with the Psalms can be a particularly powerful meditation, because the

Psalms contain everything: heartbreak and betrayal, dismay and despair, hope, healing and ultimate redemption. Within the Psalms can you pray into regaining your sense of safety and trust in God's plan for your life—which is always for your greatest good.

> Have mercy on me, O God, for men trample upon me;
>> all day long foes oppress me …
>
> When I am afraid, I put my trust in You.
>
> In God, whose word I praise,
>> in God I trust without a fear.
>>
>> What can flesh do to me? …
>
> You have kept count of my tossings;
>> put my tears in Your bottle!
>>
>> Are they not in Your book?
>
> Then my enemies will be turned back
>> in the day when I call.
>>
>> This I know, that God is for me.
>
> (Ps. 56:1-48-9)

But how do you even begin? How do you retrieve yourself from the fog created by your domestic situation and get your life back on track? How—in all the haze and daze and heartbreak, the painful disbelief and the crushing discovery of betrayal—do you "get back on track"? Can you wave a magic wand and make it all better in an instantaneous flash?

Of course, we all know healing isn't that simple, nor is it quick. The healing journey is a messy process. It takes time, and the resiliency to move through suffering.

This journey is too perilous to be taken alone—and, through the mercy and grace of our Lord, you're not alone. In the Song of Songs, the soul cries out to Jesus, her beloved Bridegroom, "Draw me in your footsteps, let us run!" (1:4) The only way to heal is to allow God to take us by the hand and draw us close, close enough so He can kiss us with His grace and love.

And then run with it. Run with His love. Let yourself release and let go. Let Him fill you with His healing fragrance (Song of Songs 1:2,3).

Just let Him.

The fastest and surest way to get back to self is to *ask*—but that's only the first step toward opening yourself to God's will. Spiritual progression is actually a four-stage process:

Ask, release, surrender, act.

Ask

There are many times in our lives when we all need to release certain things, including toxic people and circumstances. We must let go (in whatever form that may take) and shed what doesn't work in our lives so we can create the space to welcome new growth and blessings.

Often it can be difficult to let go, not because you're being asked to rid yourself of something valuable and authentic but because your habits and internal rhythms are so ingrained that it's easier to cling to the familiar than to face something new, even if the familiar is damaging. It's easy to remain stuck out of fear, forgetting that "God did not give us a spirit of fear but a spirit of power and love and self-

control" (2 Tim 1:7). Many women are too afraid to leave their abuser for financial reasons, or from the anxiety of being alone. They don't demand change because they've come to realize their husband won't change or are fearful of more rage if they even suggest such a thing. These are all very understandable and valid reasons, but even so it doesn't mean you're destined to be stuck in sorrow for the rest of your life. No one is truly stuck, no matter how dreadful their situation may seem.

Regardless of whether or not you stay in your relationship, your situation can't remain the same. Abuse can't be allowed to continue. If you need help, strength, and guidance to be able to discern your next step, how do you get that?

You need to *ask*.

It's important to become open to the knowledge that you can't do it alone. None of us can. Like everyone else, you need to become aware that *yes*, you do need supernatural help and *yes*, it is available to you. The first step is asking the Holy Spirit for the inner release to recognize your deepest needs. This will enable your spiritual path to open up in brilliant new ways.

One of Jesus' most famous teachings comes from Luke (11:9) and Matthew (7:7)—"Ask and it will be given to you ... knock and the door will be opened to you." But what is asking all about?

To ask means you have a desire: a desire to seek, a desire to change, a desire to progress, and a desire to know God on a deeper level. Where can you turn, if you don't want to be caught forever in the same cycle of abuse, year after year? Guidance and discernment are crucial. Yes, seeking professional help is essential (such as with a therapist or coach trained in abuse, a qualified spiritual director, a woman's shelter, or a support group for domestic abuse survivors). A safety plan is also needed, especially if you plan to leave—which is often when abuse and violence escalate, so extra caution, planning and protection are required (see the appendix for resources). However, seeking God through prayer is just as essential.

At this early stage *asking* takes on the pure form of belief, a belief that you'll receive once you knock, once you open the door to allow the Light of Life to stream through (John 8:12). Yet even if you don't know exactly what you're asking for, one crucial component remains true: part of your asking should always be a request to be open to divine possibility, to the light and the truth which God guarantees if you allow yourself to be filled with His goodness.

In the past, whenever I thought about the quote, "Knock and the door will be opened," I used to imagine myself standing outside, perhaps even in a cold, wintry landscape, knocking on a door so I could be welcomed into the warmth of God's presence. But what if that image is reversed?

Imagine this: You're not outside, waiting for interior entrance. Rather, the door you're knocking upon is *inside*. You're inside your own small room, and it's dark. The door is closed, locked from the outside, and you can't see anything, but you can feel your way around, and this is your saving grace. You find the door (that's always the first step). You knock. Your knock is a cry, a scream, a whimper: *Let me out, let me be free again!*

You need to get out of the prison abuse has put you in. The self-doubt, the criticism you've likely internalized, the crazy-making that has left you wondering if perhaps you truly are crazy like he says, the name-calling and belittling that has shredded your spirit and infected your soul, the rages that have left you cowering and terror-ized, the excessive jealousy and manipulative control … all these things have kept you locked in an emotional, psychological, spir-itual, and in many ways physical prison of self-isolation and bewil-derment. Abuse tends to create intense feelings of powerlessness, coupled with the shame of feeling defective. When you stand up for yourself, voice your thoughts, or insist you have rights, you're at-tacked. This wears a person down, shredding the spirit more and more as each incident occurs.

We all deserve to get out of whatever prison we may be in. We need to release and seek freedom for the health of our souls, our minds, and our entire beinghoods.

Think about it this way: since you're made in God's image and likeness, and your body is a temple of the Holy Spirit (1 Cor 6:19), then it must be a violation of Divine justice to allow abuse to con-tinue once it's recognized.

This means that through an inner commitment of prayer, you can turn from the fear of *what if?* and allow yourself to surrender to God's will. In other words, you'll feel brave enough to knock so the door will be opened as you allow God's grace to release you from your interior prison. That's one of the purposes of prayer, and one of its benefits. When you envelop yourself in the atmosphere of God's loving peace, it's easier to see the door when it creaks open.

Prayer actually helps counter the negative emotional and even physical side-effects of abuse by minimizing stress and relaxing the nervous system. Making use of brain scans, scientists have discov-ered that the left prefrontal lobes of the brain (indicating positive emotion, a peaceful state, and self-control) are activated during prayer.[43] Scott Hahn points out in his book, *Signs of Life:*

> There are many good, natural reasons to take up prayer. Physiologists recognize that they relax our bodies, reduce our stress levels, and unfurrow our brows. They also burn durable neural pathways. In every trial, God will 'provide the way of escape, that you may be able to endure it' (1 Cor. 10:13). Even amid the most extraordinary circumstances, we can escape to God, we can endure, and we can prevail, using the most ordinary means of prayer. It is a very good thing if all we need to do is touch a bead ... in order to turn our thoughts to God, because we may come to moments when that's all we *can* do.[44]

Abuse changes the map of the brain and trauma "compromises the brain area that communicates the physical, embodied feelings of being alive."[45] Additionally, "unrelenting criticism, especially when it is ground in with rage and scorn, is so injurious that it changes the

---

[43] Theresa Burke, Ph.D., "How Trauma Impacts the Brain," Rachel's Vineyard Ministries, https://rachelsvineyard.org/downloads/Canada%20 Conference%2008/TextofBrainPP.pdf

[44] Scott Hahn, *Signs of Life: 40 Catholic Customs and Their Biblical Roots* (NY, NY: Doubleday, 2009), 16-17.

[45] Bessel van der Kolk, M.D., *The Body Keeps the Score* (NY: Penguin Books, 2014), 3.

structure of the brain," which then "activates internal neural networks."[46]

However, you're not facing a hopeless situation—because of the amazing structure of the body God has created for you, new neural pathways can be created: "We can now develop methods and experiences that utilize the brain's own natural neuroplasticity to help survivors feel fully alive in the present and move on with their lives."[47] Developing an active and healthy habit of daily prayer is the most glorious way to create positive and life-affirming neural pathways that will counteract the damage done by abuse.

"Pray constantly" (1 Thess. 5:17). Prayer, when developed into a consistent practice, literally reforms the brain. Once you've established healthy patterns in your life, old habitual tendencies which no longer serve you tend to fall away as you make room for spiritual growth and inner harmony. You create the soul space for God to enter. He's eagerly awaiting your knock. He wants to open the door of your soul, to help you out of your dark room and into His merciful Light.

Many people aren't quite certain how to pray. They wonder if they should just repeat the *Our Father* or *Hail Mary* a few times (or multiple times, as in a rosary devotion), or recite some other pre-written prayer. Certainly, those forms of prayer are wonderful if that's inspiring to you. However, you should always remember that the best prayer is simply talking to God. You can—and should—speak to Him honestly and plainly, as you would a friend—because

---

[46] Pete Walker, *Complex PTSD: From Surviving to Thriving* (Lafayette, CA: An Azure Coyote Book, 2013), 91.

[47] Bessel van der Kolk, *The Body Keeps the Score*, 3.

that's exactly what He is. He's your most trusted Friend. You should also make it a habit to speak to Him often throughout your day. Ask for His help and advice. Tell Him about your day, how you're feeling, your needs and wants, and your love for Him. He's always listening and always there, even if you can't physically see or touch Him.

Some people worry about "saying the wrong thing," but that shouldn't be a concern. If your words come from an authentic purity of the heart, they're not wrong even if they're not expressed perfectly. God is your Father. No loving daddy would criticize his child's developing grammar, rejecting the child's pleas because he didn't diagram his sentences correctly (Luke 11:11—greatly paraphrased). God is wise, remember? He can see through human language. After all, He created it! You can't bungle your words with God, if you speak from the heart. That is the essence of prayer.

Frequently, throughout the day, you can recite a simple prayer in your mind, something brief and easy to remember. One prayer in particular that I find comforting and often repeat in times of high anxiety is the Divine Mercy prayer of St. Faustina, with my own little addition at the end: "Jesus, I trust in You—please help me to trust more." That's it. It's that simple. There's no need to pray with a lot of words, explanations, or beseeching; it's the energy of your soul, the inner commitment of your spirit, which God hears.

And when words fail completely, the Holy Spirit will transform your sighs and tears into prayers that will reach the heart of our Heavenly Father (Ps. 56:8, Rom. 8:26).

Release

After you've taken that first step of genuinely asking God for His help and protection, the next step is to release. But what, exactly, are you releasing?

Your expectations. Your ideal desirable outcome. Your attachments to certain things, situations—even people.

Not my will, but Yours be done (Luke 44:42).

How do you hope things will turn out in your marriage? Do you want to be done with it all, obtain a divorce and hopefully an annulment, and then get on with your life? Or would you prefer that your husband change, that somehow, miraculously, he become one of those rare abusers who experience a genuine conversion and who can admit—without blame or any excuses whatsoever—that he regularly engages in abusive behavior and he's in need of conversion and inner healing, as well as professional and spiritual help?

While it's good and even essential to pray for an abuser's authentic and lasting conversion, ultimately, he has the free will to choose whether or not to change.

Everyone's situation is unique. A subscriber to my newsletter wrote to tell me her story, and her words were so hopeful and inspirational that I want to share them with all my readers (with her permission, of course). I'm going to call her "Thérèse," because that's a beautiful name—and I'll call her husband "Ed," because that's quite generic. In Thérèse's words:

I'm from a solid Catholic background and was taught that family and marriage are sacred gifts from God. When I said "for better or worse" I meant it with all my heart, and with the certainty of my soul. My marriage was my life—not just my husband, but the five children God gave us. However, marriage was also a nightmare. Not long after our vows, Ed suddenly changed into a person I didn't even recognize. He became controlling, demeaning, belittling, and all the rest. I now recognize his behavior as textbook abuse, although it took me twenty-five years to get to that point.

When, after over twenty years of marriage, I discovered Ed had been having a long-term affair, I was devastated. I prayed constantly, trusting God would work a miracle for us. I became depressed, sure God wasn't listening, because the miracle of Ed changing never happened.

When finally I was able to hear God's answer to my prayers, it was definite and strong. He gently but firmly told me that He wouldn't fix my marriage because it wasn't a valid marriage in the first place. I heard His answer coming from deep within myself, but still I was confused. I'd spent over twenty years of dedication to Ed, and now God was telling me the marriage wasn't valid? Feeling defeated, offended, and desperate, I asked God what He meant.

His response filled me with peace, joy, and the certainty that everything would be fine. The truth, God revealed, was that in his heart, Ed never made or fulfilled his vows. "I don't want you to stay with him," I could clearly hear God telling me. "I love you. I want you out."

Those words were powerful, and brought me to tears, but I was still struggling not only to understand, but to accept this truth. As a Catholic in a sacramental marriage, how could I leave? I doubted myself and that I'd heard correctly—Ed had carefully trained me to doubt and mistrust everything about myself, and years of abusive conditioning were kicking in. I felt I must have misunderstood somehow.

But then something happened. I can't say what, exactly, except that I was given the gift of strength. Only hours after doubting myself, I suddenly found the courage to tell Ed that I wanted a divorce. I've never looked back. God has always wanted the best for me.

My life is fully God's now, without the barrier of Ed's demands, criticisms, belittling and abusive torture. I've been reborn, I've discovered my true self, I've found fulfillment and purpose. I'm now the person God created me to be. He answered my prayers—not in the way I expected, but in the best way possible.

Thérèse's story isn't unusual—specific details may be different, but our traumatic experiences of abuse and survival are the same. We are all Little Flowers, with petals broken. Yet there's always a new spring of rejuvenation and blossom, no matter how many years have passed. Spring always presents itself, again and again. St. Catherine of Siena's quote bears repeating: "If you are who you are meant to be, you will set the world on fire!"

Thérèse had to release all expectations about her situation and allow the Holy Spirit to work within her so she could accept whatever outcome He revealed. When she finally did, she found peace, joy, and the ability to move forward within God's loving embrace.

Whether you stay in your marriage or leave, when you release your personal desires and expectations, you're able to develop the ability to fully surrender to God. If you're not ready to release what you hope will be the outcome of your situation, be loving and patient with yourself and simply go back to *ask*. Ask God for the grace to want to release everything to Him. He's there for you, forever and always.

> Blessed are You, O God, with every pure blessing;
> Blessed are You because You have made me glad.
> It has not happened to me as I expected;
> but you have treated us according to Your great mercy.

(Tobit 8:15,16)

Surrender

At first glance, there doesn't seem to be much of a difference between *release* and *surrender*. It's true that the distinction is subtle, yet it's markedly there. *Releasing* is letting go of something outside of God (our expectations and personal desires), whereas *surrendering* is a falling *into* God.

When you ask God for His help and open yourself to the blessings of release, you create the space necessary within your soul to begin hearing the still, small voice of the Holy Spirit. This will truly work miracles in your life. You can begin to recapture your sense of self-confidence, joy, strength, peace and clarity of mind by acknowledging that of yourself you're nothing, but with God you're everything. St. Catherine of Siena perhaps said it best—during a mystical experience she heard the voice of God telling her: "You are she who is not; I Am He Who Is."[48]

Although it may not seem possible at this point in your life, when you ask for God's help and graces, release your personal desire and will, and surrender wholly to His plan for your life—no matter what that may be—everything will click blessedly into place. If God wants you to stay in your relationship because there's a true hope of your husband's permanent conversion, God will give you the strength, patience, and love to work on your marriage so that it reflects His vision of a sacramental union (provided your husband is doing the hard work of permanently stopping his abusive behaviors, attitudes, and core beliefs). If it's God's will that you remove yourself from a toxic relationship that hasn't changed, He will provide you with everything you need—emotional and financial support, housing, strength, courage, self-confidence, and whatever else you may require. Nothing is a quick-fix, but like the construction of a grand

---

[48] Raymond of Capua, *The Life of Catherine of Siena*, trans. Conleth Kearns, O.P. (Wilmington, DE: Michael Glazier, Inc., 1980), 91.

puzzle, each piece will lock into place in its own, Divinely-inspired time. Be patient. Don't expect overnight cures. Trust God and His timing.

We all need to have faith that, above all, in whatever situation we find ourselves, God will give us peace. Before His death Jesus promised us this peace, and He was so insistent and repetitive that we can't take His words lightly.

> Let not your hearts be troubled; believe in God, believe also in me ... Peace I leave you; my peace I give you; not as the world gives do I give to you. Let not your hearts be troubled, neither let them be afraid ...in me you may have peace. In the world you have tribulation; but be of good cheer, I have overcome the world" (John 14:1,27; 16:33).

You have to allow yourself to be open to God's glorious peace. If the devastating effects of abuse are still too overwhelming, if they're stopping you from even beginning to feel the inner joy God longs to give you, go back to *ask*. Again and again, no matter how long it takes. Healing, in order to be thorough, progresses slowly, and is always a back-and-forth progress. Acknowledge and understand your own personal healing journey, and refrain from being too critical of yourself during the "back" periods. It takes perseverance to take care of self after years—or even a lifetime—of taking care of others, but that's exactly what's needed.

Nurture yourself and give yourself the time to heal. You're worth it. After all, you're a child of God. Bask in that secure knowledge. If you let that wisdom infiltrate the core of who you truly are, you'll see yourself in an entirely different light.

The target of abuse isn't the one to be blamed. We are all children of God. We're survivors, not victims. Remember that, and be loved. Remember that, and *feel loved.*

Act

When you surrender, you're filled with the spiritual energy to act on whatever God is calling you to do.

Our Lord is a God of action and interaction, and the goal of your spiritual life should be to imitate Him as fully as you can. When you reach the stage of *act,* you're being called to become an enthusiastic participant in the shaping of Divine Will within your life. You can't expect to *ask,* then sit back and let God steer the car. You may be guided, but ultimately you have to do the driving. Think of this guidance as the Divine GPS; you'll be shown the way, but you have to grip the wheel in your own hands in order to get where we need to go. And you can be reassured that if you make a wrong turn, you'll hear the Voice within urging us to change course. *"Recalculating … recalculating …"*

I've already spoken of how essential it is to release your personal will and allow yourself to surrender to the will of God. After you *release*, you then *surrender* to the unfolding process of spiritual regeneration. This enables you to seek the help you need (spiritual, emotional, professional, and physical), the courage to move forward no matter what God wants you to do (in other words, even if it doesn't correspond with what you envisioned for your life), and the inner peace to grow toward self-love, and therefore His love. You develop discernment, the ability to differentiate your personal inner voice from the guiding Voice of the Holy Spirit.

This spiritual call to action doesn't mean you have to jump up and do something elaborate. You don't have to make immediate decisions or drastic changes just yet. Remember, healing is a slow progression. Pray and move forward when you're ready. Seek the guidance of the Holy Spirit in full charity and authenticity. Listen for discernment. Turn to trusted help. Above all, stay safe. If you have children, be sure they're well protected.

And don't feel as if you've failed if you spend weeks, months, or however long it takes on the first step of asking. Don't despair if you're not ready or equipped to act just yet. You will be. All in due time. Allow your time to be God's time, which is always perfect.

God's Will is Love

Discernment can be difficult. How can you figure out what God's will is for your life, let alone daily circumstances?

It's not quite as confusing as it may sound. God is love. That's the answer.

God's will for all of His beloved children is to experience genuine love and inner peace. I'm not talking solely about romantic love— I'm talking about living a complete, overall, and total life of love. Not the trauma of Jekyll and Hyde. Not the pain of walking on broken glass, creeping around to avoid being damaged further. Not the battering of verbal, emotional, psychological, sexual, financial, or physical violence.

Love. Just unconditional, God-like love.

The cultivation of love—nourishing others, encouraging them as they likewise encourage and support us—is God's will for your life. God desires you to lead a life full of the greatest, truest love possible.

St. Thomas Aquinas famously said, "To love is to will the good of the other."[49] That means not only do you need to will the good of others but expect the same in return.

The CCC elaborates on St. Thomas's quote by stating, "Only the good can be loved" (CCC 1766). St. Thomas reminds us not to tolerate abuse of any kind. To despise the sin of abuse and to take whatever steps you need to avoid it is one of the most powerful ways to will the good of your spouse, because it means you're no longer enabling his sinful habits by allowing the abuse to continue. "Hatred of a person's evil is equivalent to love of his good. Hence also this perfect hatred belongs to love."[50]

Any kind of abuse within the home is not to be tolerated. Ever. Whether or not your relationship can be healed depends upon many factors, and everyone's situation is different. Some women have to leave—the next chapter deals with divorce and annulment. However, there are a small number of couples who have managed to find wholeness and healing after abuse—but that depends upon whether or not the toxic behaviors and attitudes are completely and permanently eradicated. Chapter nine discusses the possibility of an

---

[49] St. Thomas Aquinas, *Summa Theologiae I-II*, Q. 26, a. 4, co., as quoted in CCC 1766.

[50] St. Thomas Aquinas, *Summa Theologiae II-II*, Q. 25, a. 6, ad. 1.

abusive personality changing his ways and becoming a man of virtue, integrity, and dependability.

Chapter Eight

If You've Had to Leave:
Exploring the Possibility of Annulment

"When our friends fall into sin, we ought not to deny them the amenities of friendship, so long as there is hope of their mending their ways ... When, however, they fall into very great wickedness, and become incurable, we ought no longer to show them friendliness."

(St. Thomas Aquinas, Summa Theologiae II-II, Q. 25, a. 6, ad. 2)

Marriages seem to be disposable in today's culture, and couples call it quits for all sorts of reasons—sometimes merely because the giddy days of first love have worn off and they get bored. The Catholic Church takes a different approach to the sacredness of marriage, going beyond the secular, "I do ... until I don't any longer." Catholics are serious about "until death do us part," truly acknowledging that, following Scriptural teachings such as Genesis 2:24 and Matthew 19:6 ("they are no longer two, but one flesh"), an indissoluble bond exists between husband and wife.

Does that mean you have to remain in a toxic and dangerous marriage? Does that mean you have to remain in a marriage even if you're being battered, controlled, verbally slaughtered, or otherwise treated as an unequal and objectified possession?

No. Let me repeat that, in case you missed it: *No.* And *no* again. Believe it or not (and this may come as a surprise to some people), remaining in an abusive union when the manipulative partner refuses to change is the opposite of what the Catholic Church teaches.

Abuse and coercive control are not aspects of an equal companionship. Respect, dignity, mutuality, and love are essential building blocks of marriage. Sacred companionship is the definition of authentic love. The opposite of sacred companionship—abuse—is corrosive, destructive, and evil.

These are the facts. Now let's get down to business.

Divorce is painful—for everyone involved. In some cases, however, it's unavoidable and necessary. If you've divorced your abusive spouse and are wondering about Church teaching on marriage and annulment hopefully some of your questions will be answered in this chapter.

Coming to terms with the possibility that your marriage was never a valid sacrament can feel harsh, painful, and confusing—especially if children are involved. Some of us don't even want to face that possibility because it's so painful. If you're one of those people, go slow, pray, and be patient with yourself. Pray for the strength to be able to make an appointment with someone in your diocese simply to discuss the possibility of a declaration of nullity. Although it can be difficult to begin, the experience can provide you with a newfound sense of freedom and relief. I personally experienced more healing during the process of obtaining an annulment than I had in traditional therapy or the best self-help books.

However, there are many questions and misconceptions about annulment, starting with the term itself. "Annulment" makes the process sound like the Church is saying your relationship never existed or that the process is merely a "Catholic divorce"—neither of which is true. A more clarifying term is *declaration of nullity* or, as Catholic author Lisa Duffy prefers, a *declaration of invalidity*.[51] What that means, and the implications it has for your past relationship as well as possible future ones, will be explained later in this chapter. What's important to remember right now is that a declaration of nullity doesn't erase your relationship as if it never existed, it doesn't invalidate your children, and it doesn't ignore all the love, sacrifice, and effort you put into your marriage. All your love and hard work remains and can never be voided.

Conditions for a Catholic Marriage

Divorce and remarriage within the Catholic Church are topics that are often misunderstood. Many people falsely believe that once married, a person can never divorce or remarry—or, if they do divorce and seek an annulment, the process will necessarily be painful, difficult, and expensive. Since these false beliefs create confusion and often more unnecessary hurt, it's time to set the record straight.

In order to marry in the Catholic Church, the couple must "freely express their consent" (CCC 1625-1629) and intend to consistently treat each other with love, dignity, and respect throughout their entire lives. Additionally, a Catholic marriage is valid only if it fits these criteria:

---

[51] Lisa Duffy, *Mending the Heart: A Catholic Annulment Companion* (Huntington, IN: Our Sunday Visitor, Inc., 2018), 37.

- Both members of the union are free to marry
- They acknowledge the permanence of marriage and intend to marry in faithfulness and fidelity, open to life and nurturing a family
- They intend the good of the other and agree to never do harm or evil to their partner; "love is patient, love is kind; love is not jealous or boastful; it is not arrogant or due" (1 Cor. 13:4-5)
- Their consent to marry is witnessed by two people before an ordained Catholic clergy member
- There is no deception between parties "concerning some quality of the other partner which by its very nature can gravely disturb the partnership of conjugal life" (CIC, Canon 1098)[52]

A sacramental marriage is indissoluble, which means it can never be broken or revoked. It's a sacred bond that has been established by God and in front of God; "they are no longer two, but one flesh" (Matt. 19:6). Regarding marriage, the *Catechism of the Catholic Church* states:

Thus *the marriage bond* has been established by God himself in such a way that a marriage concluded and consummated between baptized persons can never be dissolved. This bond,

---

[52]*Code of Canon Law*, The Holy See, http://www.vatican.va/archive/cod-iuris-canonici/eng/documents/cic_lib4-cann998-1165_en.html#CHAPTER_IX

which results from the free human act of the spouses ... is a reality, henceforth irrevocable (CCC 1640).

That's why so many people suffering in abusive marriages think *uh-oh, that means I'm stuck.*

But that's not the case.

A declaration of nullity within the Catholic Church means that a sacramental marriage failed to exist *from the beginning* of the marriage. In other words, if one or more of the above conditions don't exist at the time the wedding takes place, a true sacramental bond hasn't been formed. The confusing part about this is that many abusive personalities don't show their Mr. Hyde selves until after the wedding vows, even though this persona was there well before, lurking in the unknown shadows.

This leaves many women in psychological, emotional, spiritual, and moral anguish. After all, chances are you were filled with gushing love at the moment of your "I do" promises. You were marrying your soul mate, your Prince Charming, your best friend, the person of your dreams (or whatever romantic image best applies). Your spouse-to-be was perfect for you, mirroring your every like and dislike, a true jewel and gem and solid rock to lean on. In fact, at the time you may have been shocked that he hadn't been snatched up sooner. Perhaps he'd told tales of how many women had fallen for him, yet he hadn't loved any of them because they'd never felt right to him—until you came along. You were everything he'd ever dreamed of, and he didn't even feel worthy to be so blessed by your love, yet he was. What a miracle! You were his angel, his Godsend. Life was good!

First things first: *was* is the primary word in all this. Life *was* good but now it isn't, because the *was* proved to be false, a fairy tale. Prince Charming in his rusted armor proved to be the antagonist rather than the hero. It turned out to be a terrible plot twist, one not at all expected.

Or welcomed.

The problem with a knight in shining armor is that you can't see what's behind all that impenetrable metal. Is it a prince, or a frog?

Love-bombing is the first manipulative move in an abusive situation. It's smart and subtle, it's flattering and above all it seems innocent—and it puts the target off her guard. This first stage of the abusive set-up most often exists throughout the entire dating and engagement period. It's often not until after the vows have been solidified that the abuse cycle begins to churn, at first in a slow and creaky fashion, as if not accustomed to movement. However, the wheel soon picks up speed as the relationship progresses.

When seeking a declaration of nullity, it's important to recognize and understand the love-bombing phase of an abusive dynamic in order to recognize how your marriage "might not necessarily have been the type of marriage bond" that the true sacrament requires, and that "psychological factors which seriously impede the freedom of the party(ies)" are "grounds of nullity recognized by Church law."[53]

Even though I briefly discussed love-bombing in the first chapter, the topic is so crucial when it comes to understanding the valid

[53] Diocese of Raleigh, NC, "Freedom to Remarry: Procedures in the Diocese of Raleigh," https://dioceseofraleigh.org/sites/default/files/inline-files/Tribunal-brochure-2021-English.pdf

reasons to seek the possibility of an annulment that I want to give more details about what love-bombing is, and what it looks like. There's a fairly good chance you'll have to educate your diocese's marriage tribunal on the intricacies of domestic violence and, in particular, the earliest and most subtle stage of the abuse cycle. This education is crucial in understanding how abuse existed before the marital vows took place.

The Confusion (and Heartbreak) of Love—With an Explosion

Most likely you were love-bombed at the beginning of your relationship and most likely it felt great, creating a heady rush of intimacy. However, what most targets don't realize is that it's the motives behind the attention that matter, not the attention itself. The true purpose behind love-bombing is power and manipulation—the two core motivations of domestic abusers. The intention is to reel you in quickly and thoroughly, to encourage you to spend all your time with him instead of other potentially supportive relationships, until eventually you become dependent and easily controlled.

But then …

Dr. Jekyll turned into Mr. Hyde—either quite suddenly, in one explosive incident which then spiraled into so many you began losing count, or so covertly and insidiously that you didn't know what was happening until you were already in a state of terror and confusion. Often both are true. In any case you were likely left devastated, utterly bewildered, wholly heartbroken, and grieving.

Although you may not have been aware of it at the time of your wedding vows, the abusive part of your spouse still existed, lying dormant in wait for just the right time to emerge. Abusive parts to an individual's personality begin to form in childhood, but the toxic behaviors don't become apparent until adolescence or even later, when intimate relationships are formed. Domestic violence expert Donald G. Dutton states:

> The full development of the abusive personality may be a gradual process that occurs over years, but the path—the route by which the abusive personality creates itself—is set early on …anxious attachment (resulting from early life experiences) led to the development of an "angry temperament," which, in turn, related to attempts to control, and use abuse against, an intimate partner.[54]

In other words, abusive behaviors don't pop out of nowhere, even if it seems that way. One day your devoted, loving spouse didn't wake up and think to himself: "Hmmm. From now on I think I'll stop being loving and devoted. Instead, from now on I'll act abusively toward my dearly beloved wife. I've suddenly decided that instead of respecting her, I'm going to control her. Manipulation and mind games are fun. Why not?" Even if the signs were too covert to notice before vows were shared, the underlying dynamic of abuse was merely lying in wait during the love-bombing stage of the relationship.

Regardless of how mild the abusive and controlling behaviors begin, they increase and strengthen over time. With each new

---

[54] Donald G. Dutton, *The Abusive Personality,* 112 & 111.

boundary violation he'll push further, until you find yourself lost in a haze of anxiety, guilt, terror, and confusion.

A sacramental marriage "is made clear in the equal personal dignity which must be accorded to man and wife in mutual and unreserved affection" (CCC 1645). The sacred union is supposed to revolve around mutual self-giving and authentic companionship. Abuse, on the other hand, is chronically selfish. Obviously, this is a huge conflict.

Abusive manipulation creates an unbalanced power and control dynamic, and it doesn't allow for equal personal dignity. It's the opposite of unreserved affection. Abuse is not the picture of a mutually self-giving marriage and is a serious betrayal of the marriage vows. As Lisa Duffy points out,

> It is the betrayal of a spouse who will not or cannot change behavior that gravely hurts the health and well-being of the rest of the family. Who ever goes into a marriage relationship with the express consent to being abused or having their children abused?"[55]

If your spouse "cannot or will not" change, the Church doesn't obligate you to stay. Recall the words of the USCCB: "We emphasize that no one is expected to stay in an abusive marriage."[56] Believing you're compelled to do so isn't an act of loving neighbor or self

---

[55] Lisa Duffy, "Abusive Marriages & Divorce: What Does the Church Say?", CatholicMatch.com, https://plus.catholicmatch.com/blog/2012/08/abusive-marriages-and-divorce-what-does-the-church-say/

[56] USCCB, "When I Call for Help."

(Mark 12:31). Feeling obligated to remain in an unchanging abusive relationship isn't loving your spouse because you're enabling him to continue to abuse, and it's not loving yourself because you're not honoring the fact that you're made in the image and likeness of God (Gen 1:26) and therefore deserve to be treated with dignity, love, and respect.

Spousal abuse creates a relationship full of confusion, manipulation, and fear. The necessity of consent within the marital bond, "free of coercion or grave external fear" (CCC 1628), is essential. When consent is lacking due to the physical, emotional, or psychological coercion before the time of the wedding—even if these tactics aren't consciously recognized or acknowledged—a sacramental marriage can't take place. Consent is also lacking when someone with aggressive tendencies hides the negative aspects of his personality (whether intentionally or not) until after the vows have been exchanged. In that case you were consenting to something that didn't actually exist (CIC, 1098).[57] What you consented to was a lie, because you were unwittingly being deceived.

> For this reason (and for other reasons that render the marriage null and void), the Church, after an examination of the situation by the competent ecclesiastical tribunal, can declare the nullity of a marriage, i.e., that the marriage never existed. In this case the contracting parties are free to marry,

---

[57] "A person contracts invalidly who enters into a marriage deceived by malice, perpetrated to obtain consent, concerning some quality of the other partner which by its very nature can gravely disturb the partnership of conjugal life." (Code of Canon Law, 1098).

provided the natural obligations of a previous union are discharged (CCC 1629).

The Vatican II document *Gaudium et Spes* (*Pastoral Constitution on the Church in the Modern World*) states that "authentic married love is caught up in divine love"[58] and that's why it's sacred.

The key word in that phrase is "authentic."

"Authentic married love is caught up in divine love"—and acting abusively, coercively, and violently (regardless of what form that violence may take—physical or emotional/verbal) is not acting authentically, nor is it acting in love. It's impossible to experience authentic married love within an abusive relationship.

In marriages that had to end in divorce due to the unrepentant abuse of one spouse toward another, seeking advice on the possibility of a declaration of nullity is highly encouraged, and it's a simple process to begin—call your parish office, explain your situation, and schedule an appointment to speak to your priest.

The Church defines the married life as one in which:

- "Spouses love each other with perpetual fidelity through mutual self-bestowal."
- Is "caught up into divine love and is governed and enriched by Christ's redeeming power"
- "Leads the spouses to God … aids and strengthens them"
- "Involves the good of the whole person"
- Embodies and encourages "distinct friendship"

---

[58] *Gaudium et Spes*, 48.

- Demands "that the mutual love of the spouses be embodied in a rightly ordered manner" [59]

Does this describe your marriage? If not, and if you're now divorced, an annulment is a possibility worth exploring. Not only can it open the door to a new, healthy relationship if that's the path you feel called to pursue, but it may even prove to be a conduit to inner healing and a greater level of clarity about the level of abuse in your marriage.

Church Teaching on Domestic Abuse

The Church acknowledges the seriousness of domestic abuse and how it not only violates the marriage vow, but potentially invalidates it. Remember what the USCCB said about abuse: "As pastors of the Catholic Church in the United States, we state as clearly and strongly as we can that violence against women, inside or outside the home, is *never* justified. Violence in any form—physical, sexual, psychological, or verbal—is sinful." The USCCB goes on to state:

Some abused women believe that church teaching on the permanence of marriage requires them to stay in an abusive relationship. They may hesitate to seek a separation or divorce. They may fear that they cannot re-marry in the Church. Violence and abuse, not divorce, break up a marriage. We encourage abused persons who have divorced to

---

[59] *Gaudium et Spes*, 48,49,50.

investigate the possibility of seeking an annulment. An annulment, which determines that the marriage bond is not valid, can frequently open the door to healing.[60]

Additionally, the *Code of Canon Law* makes it clear that:

If either of the spouses causes grave mental or physical danger to the other spouse or to the offspring or otherwise renders common life too difficult, that spouse gives the other a legitimate cause for leaving, either by decree of the local ordinary or even on his or her own authority if there is danger in delay (CIC, Code 1153).

The *Canon* also states that "once the cause for separation ceases," the spouses must return to normal married life (1154). In the case of an abusive relationship, however, this often isn't possible. Abusers are notorious for promising to change, for falling back into the "love bombing" stage of the relationship, saying and doing all the right things in an effort to convince their target to return. If the relationship isn't physically or emotionally safe, and the abusive partner hasn't come to a full admittance of his toxic behaviors, if he's not making serious spiritual, psychological, and physical efforts to change (again, without excuses and blame, and taking full responsibility for his abusive personality), if he's not enrolled in a partner abuse intervention program, then the legitimate "cause for separation" still exists.

---

[60] USCCB, "When I "Call for Help."

It's also crucial to understand that if a person returns to an abusive relationship after having left, and if the toxic attitudes and behaviors haven't been healed through many years of hard work, the abuse will likely increase.

But Still ... So Many Questions! A Bit of Q&A

In the document "Catholic Response to Sexual and Domestic Violence and Abuse," the USCCB admits that education regarding domestic abuse is woefully inadequate. Their survey revealed that

> training is not often offered to marriage tribunal workers regarding domestic abuse; many workers are not trained in identifying signs of abuse and offering help, protection, and resources for abused people working through the process of a declaration of nullity (only 21% of respondents reported trained tribunal workers).[61]

Even though many advocates acknowledge that at least half of their petitioners admit to being victims of domestic violence, training in this area—including the red flags present before the marriage took place—is still uncommon. Because of this, there's a good chance that you may have to be your own advocate during the annulment process. If this is the case, educate those assisting you by

---

[61] USCCB, "Catholic Response to Sexual and Domestic Violence and Abuse," https://www.usccb.org/issues-and-action/marriage-and-family/marriage/domestic-violence/upload/Catholic-Response-to-Sexual-and-Domestic-Violence-Report-Final.pdf.

giving them books to read, sharing articles and podcasts, and talking to them honestly about what you've been through (there's a list of educational resources in the appendix). Be politely firm if you need to advocate for yourself. You're worth it.

Since there's so much misinformation and misconceptions surrounding the process of applying for a declaration of nullity, addressing the most common concerns seems to be in order. Here are some of the questions that are most often asked:

I've heard that annulments are expensive—and after my divorce, I have no money! I can't afford an annulment.

This is a common concern and an understandable one—and also, in most cases, a needless one.

On September 8, 2015, Pope Francis strongly suggested revisions to the annulment process in order to make it more approachable, and one of these changes was in regard to the potential financial burden. Pope Francis suggested that, if possible (depending upon the finances of each diocese), the process should be free of charge, and thereby available to everyone.

This change is a suggestion only, and due to the high processing costs incurred by a diocese for each request they oversee, not all dioceses have implemented Pope Francis' suggestions. However, asking for financial compensation doesn't mean a diocese is looking to make a profit off you—it's because other people need to eat and pay their mortgages. Besides the personal annulment advocate who will help you through the process, all the other people involved in deciding your case need to be paid (court officials, resource staff) as well as the cost of the business supplies and other necessary office expenses. Because of this, your diocese may ask for a fee, but the amount of the fee depends on the overhead costs the diocese will incur—and most likely your own ability to pay will be considered. For example, your diocese may ask for a donation of a few hundred dollars to cover their costs, but it's likely to be donation only. If you can't pay because your budget is tight, chances are your diocese won't refuse your request. Either they'll help you with an installment plan, or in many cases will waive the fee altogether.

This chart gives you a brief sampling of the fees charged by various dioceses and archdioceses around the U.S., as of 2022:

Diocese/Archdiocese	Fee Charged
Birmingham, AL	$200
Anchorage-Juneau, AK	None, but accepts donations.
Phoenix, AZ	Free.
Orlando, FL	Free.
Chicago, IL	$950, to be paid in full or in installments over 24 months, but "no one will be refused because of a genuine inability to pay."
Belleville, IL	$250, and "only if this is ever a serious burden to the Petitioner will the requested fee be reduced," yet "the progress of one's case or the eventual decision is never effected by one's inability to pay the full fee."

Kansas City, KS	Free. Donations accepted.
Portland, ME	$450, paid in installments or full; if unable to pay that will "in no way influence the decision of the Tribunal."
Raleigh, NC	Free.
New York, NY	$750, in full or installments, but "no one is ever turned away from the Tribunal because of an inability to pay."
Manchester, NH	Depends upon the ability of the applicant, can be free.
Steubenville, OH	Free.
Tyler, TX	Free, but a $25 filing fee is appreciated, as well as any other donation possible.
Salt Lake City, UT	$375, but "it must be understood that payment of the fee does NOT determine the outcome of the case, NOR does any inability to pay the fee prevent the case from being heard."
Seattle, WA	Free.
Washington, D.C.	Free.
Madison, WI	Free.

Milwaukee, WI	$525, paid in full or in installments; can be greatly reduced or even free if there is an inability to pay.
Cheyenne, WY	Free.

If I get a declaration of nullity, does that mean my marriage never really happened and I never had a legitimate relationship?

Again, the answer is *no*. It's important to understand that a declaration of nullity doesn't imply a secular marriage never existed, but rather that a sacred, sacramental bond was never valid in the first place. The fact that you had a civil marriage, and a true relationship in which you gave your all, will never be erased. If you're granted an annulment, that means the Church recognizes that you did everything you could to sustain a sacramental marriage, while acknowledging that for whatever reason a sacramental bond never truly took place, even though you thought it did. Your love, your effort, your devotion, your hard work and self-sacrifice will never be obliterated. It's also important to keep in mind that any children born of a marriage the Church annuls are still considered legitimate—a declaration of nullity doesn't affect their status.

I've heard that getting an annulment is difficult and psychologically grueling. Is that true? I don't need any more stress in my life!

The annulment process takes months, and sometimes a year or more, to complete. The time involved depends upon such issues as the complexity of the relationship, available marriage tribunal staff, and the promptness of respondents.

I've heard tremendous stories of healing and restoration that have been opened up and released through the process, while others have found it difficult to get through. It may take stamina, strength, and determination, or it may be a cause of immense relief. Everyone's journey is different, and the experience may depend upon how well-trained the marriage advocates are in your particular diocese. My own experience with the process of annulment was the opposite of grueling—I found it to be extremely validating and healing, and it provided closure I didn't even realize I needed. My annulment was complete in about eight months.

Yes, the questionnaire you'll receive is long and thorough, but in going through all the questions you'll be able to exam your past, all aspects of your relationship, what went wrong—and what went right. This enables you to view yourself and your decisions with more clarity, and in many cases it can help you to release any unnecessary guilt you may have been carrying around. John Miller, a reporter for the Wall Street Journal, points out, "in my entire experience of getting divorced, the church dissolution was the only time someone asked me that raw and caring question: What really happened"?[62]

If, at any time during the process, you feel overwhelmed or anxious, I urge you to go slow and honor your own individual healing journey. Many people begin the process with enthusiasm, but then

---

[62] John W. Miller, "Seeing How a Marriage Wasn't Meant to Be," Wall Street Journal, https://www.wsj.com/articles/seeing-how-a-marriage-wasnt-meant-to-be-1442531064

give up if they feel it's too difficult. Please know that you can always reach out for help. Contact your advocate, your priest, or anyone else in the diocese who can be of assistance. Find others who have successfully been through the process and speak with them. The annulment journey can produce both spiritual and emotional healing, but for some individuals this healing might be painful. Even so, in the end, it's worth the sacrifice and effort. Healing doesn't happen without discomfort, but it also bears the ripest fruit.

In most dioceses, an annulment advocate is personally assigned to each case. A properly trained advocate can help you fill out the questionnaire, answer any questions you may have, and help reassure you in times of doubt. However, as I mentioned before, this person likely isn't familiar with the tactics of domestic violence. If possible, speak to your tribunal and ask if any of the advocates on staff are familiar with your particular situation.

If there are times you feel the process to be overwhelming, take a step back and practice self-care. Small techniques can go a long way in helping you find inner peace as you travel this journey. Lisa Duffy, in her book *Mending the Heart: A Catholic Annulment Companion,* recommends five helpful things you can do if you feel emotionally overwhelmed.

- **Allow yourself to receive healing graces through the Sacrament of Reconciliation.** Why, if you're the victim of abuse and not the perpetrator? The reason why Reconciliation is so crucial is because the emotions that may be churned up during the annulment process can result in understandable feelings of anger which, if left unchecked, can lead to resentment. Justified anger can be productive and healing, but resentment always spirals on a downward path. Talking through this with a priest during the Sacrament of Reconciliation can bring tremendous clarity, peace, and graces.

- **Repeat a comforting message to yourself during times of anxiety.** When you feel overwhelmed, stressed, fearful, or full of anxiety, repeating a sacred phrase to yourself can instantly fill you with God's peace. It's a way of releasing yourself to His will, to surrendering to His desires for you, no matter what they may be. Duffy recommends St. Faustina's simple prayer of Divine Mercy, "Jesus, I trust in you!" Other options could be the Jesus prayer ("Lord Jesus Christ, Son of God, have mercy on me") the prayer from Fr. Dolingo Ruotolo's Surrender Novena ("Jesus, I surrender myself to you, take care everything") or simply, "Not my will, but Yours be done."

- **Keep a journal.** Journaling is one of the most profound ways to express any and all emotion, no matter how raw. After all, no one will see your words, and the tactile act of putting pen to paper and writing it all out is therapeutic and healing. Journaling also provides you with a reminder of your journey; as you re-read entries in the future and realize how far you've traveled, from victim to survivor, a new sense of healthy empowerment and appreciation of God's mercy in your life will begin to flow. You can also write out the full impact of your anger and negative feelings, and then burn the piece of paper in a cleansing ritual of release.

- **Pray. Then pray again.** Some individuals enjoy the tactile and peaceful repetition of the rosary, while others pick up the Liturgy of the Hours or Sacred Scripture, read a few passages, and meditate on what the words mean for them at that moment. There are many ways to pray, but all boil down to a deep communication with God and a surrendering to His will. And always remember, words aren't necessary. When words fail, the Holy Spirit will take over. "The Spirit helps us in our weakness; for we do not know how to pray as we ought, but the Spirit himself intercedes for us with sighs too deep for words." Allowing yourself to cry while acknowledging God's presence in your life is a form of prayer, too. Additionally, attending Adoration on a regular basis is one of the most powerful ways of communicating with God the Father, the Son, and the Spirit.

- **Realize that This Time in Your Life is a Gift.** Duffy points out that "now is the time to reflect on the knowledge you have acquired and how you'll allow that to shape your future decisions." Now is the time to work on yourself—not just your healing, but regaining what you feel you've lost through abuse, and triumphing in the beauty of your true self, as God created you. Did you used to have hobbies, interests, or places you enjoyed visiting which seemed to fall away as you became more and more enmeshed in your toxic relationship? Now, during this phase of self-reflection and review of your marriage, is an excellent time to reenergize those areas of your life you allowed to fall by the wayside. Create the space to become *you* again! Remember, you've been gloriously and wondrously made, and God only makes magnificent things (Ps. 139:14).[63]

I'm divorced but I haven't yet applied for an annulment. Can I still receive Communion?

There's been much confusion over the issue of divorced Catholics, so hopefully I can clarify things. In short, there's no obligation within the Church for a divorced parishioner to seek a declaration of nullity, and no prohibition against a divorced person receiving Christ in the Holy Eucharist—as long as they remain committed to living the life of a single person. As a matter of fact, receiving the True Presence of Christ in the Eucharist is a crucial way to heal your heart after the pain and trauma of divorce. As long as a person is in a state of grace and not mortal sin, receiving the Eucharist is of great blessing.

How do I begin the process for a declaration of nullity?

All you need to do to begin the process is call your local parish office and ask them what your next steps should be, or contact your diocesan Marriage Tribunal (in most cases you can get their contact information by doing an online search for "diocese of [your diocese] Marriage Tribunal"). They'll be able to point you in the right direction and provide you with the resources and information needed to get started.

---

[63] Lisa Duffy, *Mending the Heart,* 82-84.

I'm too afraid to petition for a declaration of nullity because my ex-spouse was abusive. What if he gets mad and goes after me or the children? I can't risk it.

It's crucial to explain your situation to your local Marriage Tribunal. Be forthright and open, and tell them you fear for your safety. In such a case, discretion is of utmost importance. Normally during the process of obtaining a declaration of nullity, the ex-partner will be contacted so he can also give testimony, allowing for a fuller picture of what went wrong in the marriage. If he refuses to cooperate with the process, that's fine—he has a right to decline involvement, and that will in no way affect the outcome of your request.

However, abusive marriages are a different situation. In many dioceses, your ex doesn't have to be involved in the annulment process if you make a request due to extraordinary grounds such as abuse. Your information should be kept in strictest confidence, with only a few members of the Tribunal staff having access to the documents. Ask if this is the case in your diocese and be firm about confidentiality. If you feel it may be an issue, discuss the potential of dangerous consequences should your information be leaked to your ex-abuser.

It's important for you to express your concerns and ask your priest or annulment advocate what their policies are, clarifying that your ex cannot, under any circumstances, be contacted. Talk openly and honestly about your situation and listen carefully to their responses.

Ask any and all questions that may be of concern to you.

Chapter Nine

Is He Capable or Willing to Change?

"Instead of destroying others they should be destroying the sickness within themselves."

(M. Scott Peck, *People of the Lie*)

Can someone with abusive tendencies change their attitudes and behaviors? Can they alter their lives to be Christ-centered rather than self-centered, which will enable them to understand the true meaning of a sacramental marriage?

As surprising as it may seem—and contrary to what you'll learn from many secular sources—the answer is a firm and definite *yes*. We're all given free will as a gift and grace from God. The true question isn't *can* someone change, but whether or not they're willing to go through the hard work and self-reflection required for authentic transformation.

Before I go any further, I want to repeat: if physical abuse is present in your relationship, seek safety and help. Local domestic violence shelters help women draft safety/exit plans and provide other resources on how to minimize physical risk for yourself and your children. Physical abuse usually escalates over time, particularly when the target tries to leave, which is often the most dangerous time for a victim. If this is your situation, education is important, but it's not enough. Professional advice is needed to fully protect yourself (you'll find a list of resources in the appendix).

Abuse of any kind is evil, but abusers aren't necessarily evil people. St. Catherine of Siena wrote that "every evil is grounded in selfish love of oneself. This love is a cloud that blots out the light of reason."[64] In order to truly change, the ego-driven love of self must be released, replaced with the true charity and deep humility that comes only from God.

Types of Abusers

Not all individuals who use abuse to control their relationships do so with the same motivations. Even though tactics and techniques often follow the same pattern in many toxic relationships, the underlying causes for mistreatment vary (and remember, causes are not the same as excuses). For example, Lundy Bancroft claims abusive behavior is a conscious choice, whereas Donald G. Dutton, professor of psychology at the University of British Columbia and director of the Assaultive Husbands Program in Vancouver, has observed from research and neurobiology, as well as from analyzing the characteristics of certain personality disorders, that "the simplistic notion that all abuse perpetrators *choose* to be abusive is contradicted by the work on subtypes and on impulsivity."[65]

---

[64] St. Catherine of Siena, *The Dialogue*, 103.

[65] Lundy Bancroft, *Why Does He Do That? Inside the Minds of Angry and Controlling Men*; Donald G. Dutton, *The Abusive Personality: Violence and Control in Intimate Relationships, 2nd Edition*, 15.

The reason some authors claim all abusers are narcissistic manipulators who purposely mistreat their partners is because they're focusing on a certain type of perpetrator rather than differentiating between the four basic subtypes. In a very simplistic nutshell, the four types of abusive personalities are:

- Generally violent/antisocial
- Family only
- Dysphoric/borderline
- Low-level antisocial

The "generally violent aggressor" is not only violent to his intimate partner but to others outside the home, and it's not unusual for them to have a criminal record. These types of aggressors may have full-blown antisocial personality disorder or be a sociopath or psychopath. They're completely devoid of empathy and share no authentic feelings of remorse, although they may pretend to be apologetic and feign empathy to get what they want or to stop their victim from leaving. The "generally violent aggressors" intentionally use violence to hurt people, particularly but not limited to their partners. This type of personality is a master at coercive control and is most often physically and sexually violent, feeling no qualms about raping their partners or committing other horrific deeds.

It's unlikely a "generally violent aggressor" will change. These types of individuals simply don't respond to therapy, if they'll even go at all—quite often the only reason they attend is because a court mandated it. If they're forced to attend group sessions, they're often disruptive to other members. They like themselves the way they are and see nothing wrong with their behaviors. They can't live without power and control over others.

To outsiders, the "family only" aggressors are gems—exceptionally nice, considerate, ambitious, respectful. They seem like the type of guy anyone would be lucky to marry—but buyer beware. Behind closed doors, they're different people altogether. In the home environment, the "family only" aggressors tend to be impulsive and, if physically abusive, are more apt to slap their partners rather than using fists or other weapons. These abusers are "the least likely to engage in psychological and sexual abuse,"[66] and their abusive episodes are infrequent rather than cyclical, tending to occur on an average of six times a year.

Happily, these types of abusers—if determined and willing to go through the long, hard work necessary—can make positive improvements in behavior. Catholic clinical psychologist Dr. Christauria Welland has worked extensively with men in programs designed to change their abusive ways. Despite her success with these programs, she emphasizes that change is rare unless there's an extended intervention to transform not only abusive behaviors, but attitudes, thought processes and judgements. About the "family only" aggressors she states, "If they want to, they can really make some important

---

[66] Amy Holzworth-Munroe and Gregory L. Stuart, "Typologies of Male Batterers: Three Subtypes and the Differences Among Them," https://psych.indiana.edu/documents/holtzworth-munroe-and-stuart-1994.pdf.

changes in their therapy and really do much better with their families. They usually have fewer psychological problems."[67]

Those in the "dysphoric/borderline" category tend to be emotionally unstable and are haunted by extreme jealousy and a deep-rooted fear of abandonment due to their underdeveloped sense of self. These types of personalities are termed "borderline" because of what seems to be multiple personas—in public they're charming, successful, and often free with donating time or money to others. However, in private they tend to be emotionally explosive, depressive, and cyclical in their behavior. These are the types of personalities that, according to research and statistics, are more likely to commit murder/suicide when their partners plan to leave or actually make their exit from the relationship, especially if they've been physically abusive in the past.[68] Their intimate relationships are highly unstable because they tend to undermine their partners by using tactics of severe gaslighting, as well as verbal and psychological attacks. "Dysphoric/borderline" is the most common type of abuser and represents those who abuse in a cyclical manner (see chapter one for information on the abuse cycle).

As with "family only" abusers, "dysphoric/borderline" personalities can change—as long as they can commit to years of hard work,

[67] Christauria Welland, Psy.D., "Violence and Abuse in Catholic & Christian Families: Preparing an Effective and Compassionate Pastoral Response."

[68] Dorothy and Steve Halley, "Cracking the Code: Understanding the Different Motives of Those Who Batter," online course, Family Peace Initiative, https://fpiacademy.thinkific.com/courses/cracking-the-code-understanding-the-different-motives-of-those-who-batter.

determination, and an authentic desire to transform their lives. They must be willing to embrace the challenge and invest the time into becoming better, virtuous people. They'll have to learn how to develop empathy, be compassionate, engage in active listening, and understand other people rather than focusing solely on themselves.

The "low-level antisocial" personalities are similar to the "generally violent aggressors," but they're not as extreme. Because of this, these types of people may be more open to treatment, but again this is rare and will take a great deal of very difficult work as well as extreme, life-altering change. As with the "dysphoric/borderline," they'll have to reframe their entire lives and learn, with professional help, how to not only behave differently, but how to develop virtuous thinking skills and to transform their attitudes.

The conclusion to all this is that if we're not talking about a "generally violent aggressor" who is unlikely to make any improvement in his behavior, and if the fear of physical violence is not an issue, then the answer to "can he change" is *yes*. Yes, but …

Change is possible, yet it's extremely difficult and requires a permanent determination. I like to think of St. Paul as the patron saint of men willing to turn from their destructive behaviors and transform their lives. He persecuted Christians—even to the point of death—yet through the grace of God he completely transformed his life, publicly renouncing his former attitudes, beliefs, and actions. If your spouse can do that, in authenticity and humble confession, then there's hope.

Change is possible, but …

Authentic change must begin with a foundation of humility—and that's one thing most people with heavy narcissistic traits can't tolerate. Humility, honesty, openness, and a willingness to confess each and every abusive behavior and attitude are crucial components of change.

An individual who has used abuse to control his relationship needs to acknowledge his actions and manipulations. He has to own them, admit them, and be determined to reform them. He has to fully confess, in all honesty and without excuse or blame—to you, to anyone else he's abused, and to a priest through the Sacrament of Reconciliation.

In order for an individual to transform his life he has to find the Road to Damascus, get on it, and walk. And keep walking all the way to the end, despite the enticing detours and exhaustion that may tempt him to turn back. He can't remain in his delusional world of power-over, control, twisted mind games, blaming and excuses. Those behaviors indicate he's still on the delusional Yellow Brick Road, not the Road to Damascus.

In Acts chapter 9 we read about the abuser Saul, a persecutor of Christians and a man complicit in murder. He hated the followers of Christ and sought to purge them from the world.

But then something happened. Something immense, something dazzling, a soul-expanding experience that left Saul prone on the ground with newly awakened love, humility and understanding. On the Road to Damascus, Saul the abuser began his journey toward becoming St. Paul the Apostle:

Saul, still breathing threats and murder against the disciples of the Lord ... approached Damascus, and suddenly a light from heaven flashed about him, and he fell to the ground and heard a voice saying to him, 'Saul, Saul, why do you persecute me?' And he said, 'Who are you, Lord?' And he said, 'I am Jesus, whom you are persecuting; but rise and enter the city, and you will be told what you are to do'" (Acts 9:1,3-6).

After his Road to Damascus conversion experience, St. Paul used his God-given free will to authentically remove the abusive patterns in his life to completely reform. He gave up his control, his power, and his position, all for Christ.

The Yellow Brick Road is a different path altogether. This is the path of distortion and illusion. At the end of the road there is no salvation, no conversion, no hope. Instead, a small man is revealed, someone hiding behind an ego-driven curtain who in truth holds no power, not even over himself.

The Road to Damascus is the road to clarity, honesty, and self-examination. For a man to become a truly self-giving spouse, he has to fully acknowledge his abusive behaviors—all of them. He can no longer try to gain your empathy with victimhood stories such as "well, it was my rotten childhood," or "my ex was crazy and cheated on me"—which are two of the most typical excuses.[69] If your spouse

---

[69] See Bancroft, *Why Does He Do That?*, 25-29. Additionally, I've spoken with countless women in support groups and various other private settings, and nearly all of them have reported their abuser repeatedly told them stories of "childhood abuse" and "ex abuse/cheating," citing these issues as reason for their own abusive behavior. However, as Lundy

is still in denial or making excuses he's not changing, no matter what he may claim.

Again, in order to authentically and permanently change—and the only way you should begin to *slowly* and *carefully* trust him again, through the guidance of the Holy Spirit and deep prayer—is if he experiences a true conversion. I'm not talking about mere words or promises to get help, but an authentic spiritual conversion. St. Thomas Aquinas wrote:

> The soul is the life of the body, and God is the life of the soul … When charity is lost, the soul is said to be deformed … It is necessary that there be some habit of charity created in the soul, according to which the Holy Spirit is said to dwell in the soul itself.[70]

Bancroft wrote, "A non-abusive man doesn't use his [childhood] past as an excuse to mistreat you. Feeling sorry for your partner can be a trap, making you feel guilty for standing up to his abusiveness … the instant he uses [his ex-partner] as an excuse to mistreat you, stop believing *anything* he tells you about that relationship and instead recognize it as a sign that he has problems with relating to women," 27 & 29. See also Hennessy, *How He Gets Into Her Head,* 32-33; Joseph M. Carver Ph.D., "Love and Stockholm Syndrome: The Mystery of Loving an Abuser," http://drjoecarver.makeswebsites.com/clients/49355/File/love_and_stockholm_syndrome.html, who sums up this behavior, "Personality disorders and criminals have learned over the years that personal responsibility for their violent/abusive behaviors can be minimized or even denied by blaming their bad upbringing, abuse as a child … 'sad stories' are always included in their apologies—after the abusive/controlling event …"

[70] Thomas Aquinas, *In I Sent,* d. 17, Q. 1, a. 1, arg. 2; 1, s.c. 1; s.c. 3).

Your partner has to work his way back to true charity, to the un-bending of his soul, to spiritual health and wellbeing, to genuine conversion. He has to humbly take the four necessary steps which I described in chapter seven: *ask, release, surrender* and then *act*. And act appropriately, in true love.

This is a very long process. It can begin with a sudden realization, but it's not a sudden fix. It'll take years of extremely difficult, self-reflective work, including prayer, spiritual guidance and a complete restructuring of his attitudes and thought processes. It'll take immense patience on his part—and yours, if you're willing. And if you're not willing, the main thing to remember is that you're a child of God who deserves love and respect, not abuse.

Self-care through the guidance of the Holy Spirit is crucial. Change will require him to develop and maintain patience, perseverance, and love. To again quote St. Paul, "Love is patient and kind; love is not jealous or boastful; it is not arrogant or rude. Love does not insist on its own way; it is not irritable or resentful" (1 Cor. 13:4-5). If any of those things are lacking in his attitude or behavior, then no real progress is being made, no matter what he may claim with mere words. Dr. Christauria Welland cautions, "Learning how to be non-violent is a specific set of skills [that cannot be achieved] unless he gets domestic violence counseling."[71]

A list of necessary criteria for initiating change include:

---

[71] Christauria Welland, "Violence and Abuse in Catholic & Christian Families."

- Full confession of his abusive behavior in all its forms, without any excuses, blame and minimizing. He has to admit to you all his faults, all lies, and everything he has kept hidden—in other words, every aspect of his behavior. If he tries to explain with any excuses whatsoever, or any form blame-shifting, that's a sure sign he's not changing.

- He needs to recognize and authentically apologize for specific incidences in which he can now recognize he had been acting abusively—not generalizations, but the actual events and what he did that was abusive and damaging to you.

- Accept and admit that his abusive behavior is evil and a violation of your personhood. We are all made in God's image, and our bodies are temples of the Holy Spirit (Gen. 1:26; 1 Cor. 6:19). Abuse doesn't "glorify God in your body" (1 Cor. 6:20) but rather the opposite. The abusive man isn't just violating you, he's violating the temple of the Holy Spirit. He needs to fully realize and admit that.

- Complete recognition of the devastating effects the abuse has had on you and maintain consistent empathy toward your healing process. No matter how long it may take for you to heal, to trust him and to want to be close to him again, he can't complain or try to rush you. If he gives you a time limit (for example, saying he expects you to be "over it" in a merely a few months), then he's not changing. He can't violate your boundaries any longer. Remember, "love is patient and kind."

- Self-reflection and prayer will be necessary for your partner to recognize all of his controlling attitudes and behaviors, as well as the ways in which he feels entitled.

- Make full reparation to everyone he has hurt, damaged, or betrayed.

- Stop all talk of being a "victim" and blaming his victimhood status on his abusive actions and attitudes. Playing the victim is a primary tactic of abusers, but whether or not he's endured a rough childhood or other forms of trauma is a non-issue. Again, *there is no excuse for abuse.*

- Acknowledge that his abusiveness was an act of his own free will and not caused by something external to him.

- Empathy, respect, equality, non-judgmental communication skills, and a complete change in attitude will need to be established in order for true change to take place.

- Recognize and replace his twisted thinking and the ways he's distorted his beliefs about you, your relationship, and about your past together.

- Develop the determination not to repeat any abusive behaviors—and he must stick to that promise.

- Discontinue all friendships with toxic people. If he has unhealthy companions, they shouldn't be his friends any longer.

- Fully respect your boundaries—at all times.

- Admit that his healing and change won't happen overnight, that in fact it could very well be a life-long process. Like an alcoholic twenty years sober, every day of his life he'll have to be on his guard to consciously decide not to abuse,

control, deceive and manipulate others. He has to continu-
ally work on himself and ensure that he never again says or
does anything abusive toward you or anyone else.

Every one of these criteria must be consistently and thoroughly
met over a long period of time before trust and intimacy can begin
to be rebuilt. If your husband isn't willing to be patient and determined, and if he's not empathetic to your process of healing, then he
hasn't even begun the process of conversion. He must also understand that you won't be able to trust him again until change has been
definitely established over a long period of time (years, not days or
even months). "Every offense committed against justice and truth
entails the *duty of reparation,* even if its author has been forgiven"
(CCC 2487).

The Road to Damascus vs. the Yellow Brick Road

The Road to Damascus is defined by an openness to divine revelation. It's a complete conversion through the grace of the Holy
Spirit and the power of Christ, rooted in the protection of the Father
and guided by an individual's determination to make the necessary
changes. The Road to Damascus is also the road to humility and acknowledgment of the hard work to come. Dr. Christauria Welland
is firm on what an abuser needs to do to reform:

He needs to get a specific set of tools: tools in his mind, tools
in his behavior … That takes time, that takes *work,* and of
course it takes motivation. It can be done, but it's not going

to happen randomly, and it's not going to happen just because the person comes back to God.[72]

The Yellow Brick Road is the opposite of the Road to Damascus. It's a choice and a conscious decision to remain on a path that ultimately leads to a "man behind the curtain" who is no god, but rather a weakened vessel pretending to be something he is not.

Is it wrong continue hoping your spouse will become loving and kind, even to the detriment of self? Most abusers don't change. That's a sad harsh truth—and one that's difficult to admit—but it's a truth nonetheless. It's not that they're incapable, but more that they don't want to go through the difficult task of self-reflection and the humility required to admit their sins. A recovering abuser once told me, "The most difficult thing I've ever had to do was admit that I was wrong—about everything." That admittance takes enormous strength, perseverance of character, and accepting grace from the Holy Spirt.

Most abusers prefer to remain in their delusions, their positions of control, manipulation, and power-over—all of which derive from low self-esteem and shame. They can't let go, because if they do they'll feel too vulnerable. Yet we're all vulnerable in love—that's what self-giving is all about, and that's the beauty of it. To an individual who has spent a lifetime clinging to their negative behaviors, however, this vulnerability isn't a gift of love, but a detriment. They

---

[72] Christauria Welland, "Violence and Abuse in Catholic & Christian Families."

remain wandering on the Yellow Brick Road, with nothing but more delusion at the end.

Yet not all abusers remain on the Yellow Brick Road. It takes a lifetime of struggle to overcome a lifetime of destructive patterns, but through cooperation with God's grace it can be done. If a person can overcome his abusive tendencies and gain the courage to resist manipulating his loved ones, he's just stepped off the Yellow Brick Road and begun his journey on the Road to Damascus.

The journey toward authentic change is difficult, frustrating, and often painful for all parties involved. Always remember, God is with you on this uncomfortable journey, regardless of whether your spouse does his work to become the partner you deserve. Have faith and trust in God, especially when you feel there's no one else you can trust. "When I am afraid, I put my trust in You. In God, whose word I praise, in God I trust; I shall not be afraid" (Psalm 56:3-4).

The Art of Deception

Change is raw. It's a stripping away, a revealing of complete inner vulnerability and naked honesty—things difficult to achieve for someone who has spent years, decades, or a lifetime in deceit.

Manipulative people lie. It's what they do to get away with their actions. They lie so naturally that they even lie to themselves and truly come to believe their own concocted stories. "The lie is designed not so much to deceive others as to deceive themselves. They cannot or will not tolerate the pain of self-reproach."[73]

---

[73] M. Scott Peck, *People of the Lie*, 75.

Yet if they refuse to tolerate the pain of self-reproach, change will continue to be impossible. There may be an appearance of change, but that will be temporary, and the abuse will eventually return, usually worse than before. Permanent change can't happen without the intense pain of intense self-reflection and even more intense self-honesty. This is a very difficult task for someone unaccustomed to honesty, but the only other alternative is for the abuser to remain mired in his destructive habits, his soul dragged down by his personal actions and sinful choices.

Another thing to keep in mind is that when a person authentically admits to a lie, they'll feel remorse, guilt, and shame. They'll apologize—willingly, without being coerced into it, and without blame or excuse—and they'll change their ways. If your husband admits to a lie after you insist on the truth yet then says, "but I didn't tell you because I knew you'd get mad," "it wasn't a big deal," "I forgot," or any other excuse he may come up with, he's showing no pain or remorse, and is only fessing up because he got caught. He may be sorry he got caught, but he's not sorry for what he did. That's hardly true remorse.

Above all else, though, be on your guard and don't forget that individuals who resort to abuse as a means of control know how to lie, and they know how to lie well. They'll deny what they did so vehemently that you'll begin to doubt what you know to be true, even if you have concrete proof. They may feign an apology, and appear thoroughly genuine, but even that might not be authentic.

Because of this, the person who acted abusively toward you isn't to be trusted until he's been on the Road to Damascus for a very long and consistent time. He must also recognize and admit the truth about his habit of lying and secrecy.

The *Catechism of the Catholic Church* clearly outlines the seriousness of lying to others:

> The *gravity of a lie* is measured against the nature of the truth it deforms, the circumstances, the intentions of the one who lies, and the harm suffered by its victims. If a lie in itself only constitutes a venial sin, it becomes mortal when it does grave injury to the virtues of justice and charity. By its very nature, lying is to be condemned. It is a profanation of speech … The deliberate intention of leading a neighbor into error by saying things contrary to the truth constitutes a failure in justice and charity … Since it violates the virtue of truthfulness, a lie does real violence to another. (CCC 2484, 2485, 2486).

Lies come in many forms. They can be direct or indirect, in the guise of outright misinformation, half-truths or evasions. They can also take the form of "word-salad," when a manipulator craftily spins words into a confusing jumble to confuse his target so thoroughly that out of sheer exhaustion she decides to believe him. After all, it's easier that way.

In other words, lies, like sins, are those things we have done, and those we've failed to do.

It's also crucial to keep in mind that manipulative people are keen listeners. They often don't seem to be because they supposedly—and conveniently—"forget" so much, or deny you said something you know you said (or did). Yet that's all a trick, too. In reality, they listen closely to what you say and act accordingly, depending on what they want from you. They'll use what they learn by listening to your needs, desires, preferences, and aversions. This is to their ultimate benefit, because all this information enhances their lying skills. They've learned just the right things to say and do to get you to believe them. With a straight and seemingly humble face they'll look you in the eye and lie, deny, blame, and excuse away their deceptive behavior. They'll persist until they get their way, and you cave in, buying their excuses once again.

Without trust, where does a marriage stand? On a sandy foundation, at best.

The essence of lying is not merely deceiving others but hiding from ourselves. Evil was first introduced into God's perfect world first through sin, and second through attempting to hide from that sin. In chapter two I compared the fall of man in the book of Genesis with the evils of abuse. Going a step further into the mythological story, Adam and Even betrayed their Creator through disobedience, introducing the original sin that was to infect their gene pool and all future generations. Then, ashamed at their foul deed, "the man and his wife hid themselves from the presence of the LORD God among the trees of the garden" (Gen. 3:8). To hide from God is to hide from self. To evade the inmost self that is made in the image and likeness of God is to give in to evil, "for evil is the absence of the good that is natural and due to a thing," as St. Thomas Aquinas said.[74] God is natural to us; He is the most natural part of our entire beinghood. The absence of God, evading Him so as not to have to face our own

---

[74] St. Thomas Aquinas, *Summa Theologiae I,* Q. 49, a. 1, co.

sinfulness and selfishness, is to create a void in the soul. All voids must be filled with something. If not filled with Truth and God, then what will fill that deep inner vacuum caused by evasion of self and evasion of God? It was none other than Jesus who answered that question.

> When the unclean spirit has gone out of a man, he passes through waterless places seeking rest; and finding none he says, 'I will return to my house from which I came.' And when he comes he finds it swept and put in order. Then he goes and brings seven other spirits more evil than himself, and they enter and dwell there; and the last state of that man becomes worse than the first" (Luke 11:24-26).

I mention the abuser's skill in lying not to discourage you, but to make you aware so you can be on your guard, fully alert to the potentials of further deception.

There can be no authentic change without God. The grace of the Sacrament of Reconciliation is absolutely essential. If your spouse isn't willing to bare his soul to a priest, then he isn't going to change.

Even if he does incorporate God into his healing, this still isn't enough. Many individuals with abusive tendencies use religion as a manipulative tool, abusing Sacred Scripture (see chapters five and six) or putting on a piously pharisaical face to get others to believe he's devout. Religious conversion is necessary, but it must be authentic and can never be used as a means of further manipulation.

One of the most crucial things he needs to do is to enter domestic abuse group counseling—not general therapy, but counseling specifically for the domestic abuser with a therapist highly trained and experienced in this field. Anger management classes, substance abuse counseling and spiritual direction are things that can come later. Specific domestic abuse counseling, in a peer group setting, is what is necessary as a first essential step.

I can't stress this enough: To change, an individual must be willing to attend a qualified abuser's intervention group program and stick with it for the duration of the program period, attending and actively participating in every meeting. This program must involve the victimized partner by keeping her up-to-date on her spouse's progress—whether he's showing up for meetings, as well as their general assessment of his attitudes, changes and behaviors. A good place to find a qualified program is to ask for recommendations from your local domestic violence shelter. Make sure to research the qualifications of the leaders of the program, find out exactly what will be taught and how, and any other questions you may have.

I also recommend that he work on the part of himself that feels the need to express itself abusively, which can be done through a therapeutic modality called Internal Family Systems (IFS). Finding a qualified Christian IFS counselor or coach can be truly life changing; in the appendix, I've recommended a few resources to help you learn more about IFS.

It's also crucial to keep in mind that couples counseling is not recommended. This type of counseling is for non-abusive couples only—those who have problems communicating, can't agree on parenting methods, or any other typical marital issue. Abuse isn't a marriage issue—it's an abuser issue. It's also not a communication problem, since manipulative personalities aren't interested in authentic conversation, but only in being right and being in control. Marriage counseling does more harm than good in abusive relationships, because the manipulative partner will likely charm the therapist while placing the blame on you, failing to take responsibility, and using circular talk as a coercive technique to make himself sound credible. When one partner continuously disrespects, abuses, minimizes, and belittles the other, marriage counseling will only re-traumatize the target.

Always keep in mind that abusers aren't inherently evil. They, like the rest of us, are made in the image and likeness of God. It's up to them to see this, realize this, change the nature of their abusive ways, and not let themselves fall so far into their sin that they can't even see the need to get out.

St. Catherine of Siena pointed out that "the soul cannot stand still; she has either to advance toward virtue or turn back ... Anything worthwhile calls for perseverance ... perseverance is essential if you want to see your desires realized."[75]

Yet we must face the possibility that this may never happen. The transformation from an abusive person to a trustworthy, loving spouse can, and does, take place, but oftentimes a manipulative personality doesn't want to go through the immense work it takes to travel this path of healing and transformation. This is a possibility all individuals in abusive relationships must come to terms with, through prayerful discernment. Sometimes, we must face the truth and stop waiting for our fairy-tale ending. Sometimes there is no *happily ever after*.

---

[75] St. Catherine of Siena, *The Dialogue*, 130, 101.

Then again, sometimes there is.

A Repentant Soul's Prayer to Saint Paul

St. Paul, I need your intercession. I want to walk the Road to Damascus with you. On this journey, our Lord and Savior changed the entire course of your life. You were an abusive man, persecuting Christ's beloved followers, but He shook the scales from your eyes and revealed His truth to you. I ask Him to change the course of my life beginning today.

I understand now that when I violate the dignity of others, especially those whom God has entrusted to my care, I violate Christ Himself. In His mercy, may He remove the scales from my eyes. May He heal me, reveal His truth to me, and shower me with His Divine Mercy.

Through the cleansing Blood of Christ and His most Merciful Heart, I pray for your help and guidance, St. Paul, as I travel my own Road to Damascus. May I become the whole, healed, and authentically loving man, husband, father, and child of God I was created to be. In Jesus' name I pray. Amen.

(written by Jenny duBay and Laura Ercolino of Hope's Garden)

Chapter Ten

Grief, Healing, and the Triumph of Recovery

*"Judas came, one of the Twelve, and with him a great crowd with
swords and clubs. And he came up to Jesus at once and said,
'Hail, Master!' and kissed him."*

(Matt. 26:47,49)

Intimate partner violence is a betrayal—of trust, of relationship, of perceptions and promises. It's a violation of all you held close to your heart, and as a result it's a serious trauma. The main effects of trauma are disconnection from self and others, and a sense of debilitating loss of … well, everything.

Or so it feels.

Despite what may seem like the overwhelming immensity of your emotions and the topsy-turvy curve to their unpredictability, recovering from your trauma is a journey that's not as overwhelming as it may at first seem. Healing takes time and patience, but not only is it possible, it will ultimately reveal beautiful layers of strength and resilience you never realized you had.

I understand where you're at. Chances are, your world has shattered. It may feel as if everything you held to be true has suddenly proven false. When you've trusted someone beyond all measure, with dreams for a future of mutual self-giving and authentic love, the dissolution of that dream creates a hard fall.

How can a person recover from such damage, shock, and blatant misuse of what should be a loving and trusting relationship? Once you come to the realization that *yes, this is abuse* and something has to change, how do you move forward? Likely you feel battered—even if he's never physically touched you. You may feel as if you're existing in a hazy fog; confused, anxious, depressed, hopeless, fearful … How do you begin to build your new beginning after so much pain?

Self-Care

Throughout the healing journey, your focus needs to be on self-care.

Although you may feel frozen and helpless, the best way to begin the climb back to your true self by talking about your situation rather than keeping it bottled up inside. However, I urge you to be careful about this. Not all people are safe to talk to, and unfairly slandering your partner is never a good idea. Despite the justified hurt you may feel, retaliation is unproductive and damaging to everyone involved.

It's crucial to find empathetic loved ones who can relate—perhaps they, too, have been through a betrayal trauma. When seeking professional help, make sure any coach or therapist you contact is experienced in whatever trauma you're facing. If you're not sure, ask. Send an email or make a phone call. Don't be afraid to inquire about specific qualifications and why a particular professional may (or may not) be a good fit for you.

Even simply talking with friends over a cup of coffee is extremely helpful. However, I recommend that these individuals are *your* friends, not mutual friends between you and your spouse. And, again, a vetting process is in order. Are these safe people to talk with? Will they truly understand, or will it end up being more damaging and traumatic for you to confide in them?

It's also important not to judge or criticize yourself. You're not to blame for what's happened, and reactions of fear, anxiety, self-isolation, and confusion are normal. To regain your balance and renew your soul after the painful trauma you've endured, you need to feel safe again. You can begin creating a safe space within yourself by doing whatever it is you need to do to remain sane and begin the path toward healing—as long as those things are healthy and helpful.

Some suggestions for self-care during this critical time of crisis include:

- Make sure you're getting enough sleep. Adequate sleep is essential for mood regulation.
- Listen to music, especially songs and artists you used to love, but haven't listened to since your life changed. Better yet, make a playlist of all your favorite and empowering songs and name it "Freedom."
- Eat well—healthy whole foods, nourishing dishes. Junk in the body creates junk in the mind.
- If you like animals, spend time with them. Pets are non-critical, loving, and they relieve stress. If you don't have a pet yourself, consider visiting your local humane society or

animal shelter and spending time with animals who need love as much as you do.

- Exercise, in whatever form you prefer—that may be kickboxing or MMA, weight training, running, walking, stretching routines, etc.

- Do what brings you peace, joy, and a sense of fulfillment. If you don't know what that is any longer because of a serious loss of self, think back to what you used to enjoy in your pre-trauma days. Then, *do that.*

- Develop a solid prayer life. This can include Christian meditation, a rosary devotion, the Liturgy of the Hours, and/or a deep practice of personal communication with God throughout your day.

- Be patient with yourself. Be loving. Be gentle. Be understanding. You've been through a lot. Healing takes time—a lot of time. It's okay. You can do it, but within your own time. Allow yourself that time.

As you move through the initial stage of crisis, you may find your mind bargaining with itself. "What if" and "if only" scenarios may play and replay in your head to the point of exhaustion: *What if he changes? Is he changing? What if I'm to blame or did something wrong? If only this had never happened ... If only he were different ... If only I'd never done* [fill in the blank] ...

This is common, but unproductive. When you find yourself falling into these thought-holes—questions that have no answers and aren't healthy to ruminate over—go back to the list of self-care options and try to focus more on yourself and your needs rather than the one who betrayed you. You can think about relationship questions at a later stage in your healing. For now, *self-care* is of primary importance.

If you've felt numb or disconnected—a common unconscious way of dealing with recurring abuse—you may find emotions returning as you begin a healthy self-care routine. Although painful, this part of the journey is also normal, necessary, and extremely beneficial. Being able to feel again means being able to feel joy as well as pain, peace as well as anxiety. As you move through the process, the negative effects of trauma will begin to steadily decrease and eventually disappear altogether.

During this stage you'll likely find yourself in a state of grief and mourning. Allow this to happen. When you allow grief to enter, through the pain of recovery, you open the doors for true healing to begin. Regardless of whether you're still with your spouse, grief is an essential aspect to healing. You're mourning a loss—the death of what you thought your relationship had been, the death of your future dreams, the death of a love you imagined existed. Mourning takes time and can't be rushed.

Grief, Mourning, and Ultimate Healing

When a close friend of mine was a teenager, he was involved in a devastating auto accident that nearly took his life. Despite the crumpled mess of his car, despite the fact that his windshield was shattered on the asphalt because he'd been hurled through it, despite the fact that *he* was shattered on the asphalt, wrecked next to the wreckage, he felt little if any pain. His entire body was in shock, and he soon became unconscious due to the extent of his injuries.

It wasn't until later, safely stabilized, operations complete, lying in hospital recovery, that the agony hit him. And it hit hard. The path to healing was excruciating, yet it was also necessary. If he hadn't felt pain, that would have meant he was paralyzed and would never walk again. If he hadn't felt the pain, something would have been seriously, tragically wrong.

The only present-day reminders of such a traumatic experience are scars which have now faded into barely noticeable white marks on his skin. These are the reminders of his determination, what he endured, and what he overcame. They're battle scars of strength.

Healing is like that. Thawing from the effects of trauma is a painful process. Allowing those battered and numbed emotions to come to life again—welcoming the grief to enter—can feel overwhelming at times. Yet if you don't feel the pain, that means you're paralyzed. If you don't feel the pain, that means there's something seriously, tragically wrong. If you don't face your pain head-on, if you try to avoid it, you're delaying the inevitable—and in the long run, you'll end up causing yourself more suffering.

It's helpful to put a name to what you've lost. Write down what you thought you had in your relationship—examples can include friendship, trust, unconditional love, safety, honesty, acceptance, joy, fun, and so much more. Write down any and all of it—the good, the bad, and the in-between. Then, when you feel ready, look over your list and, one by one, release your expectations of *what could have been* to make room for *what is now*.

Does this mean you have to give up all hopes of future joy or safety, friendship or fun? Definitely not—in fact, by releasing the internal images of what you thought you'd had, you'll open the way for true joy to enter: joy, peace, inner contentment and self-companionship. By acknowledging the illusion caused by intimate partner violence, you'll release clinging hopes for what could have been in order to make room for a stronger and more fulfilled life.

Even if you're one of the few people whose spouse now authentically accepts that he's been abusive and says he's willing to change, letting go of what you thought your relationship had been is essential to your inner growth and healing. You have to start again, from a healthy place. This is true if you stay in the relationship, or if you decide to leave.

To build stronger and healthier future goals, you must mourn the death of what you thought your life was going to be. "Blessed are those who mourn, for they shall be comforted" (Matt. 5:4).

Trying to force or coerce a situation to make it what you want it to be will only result in more heartbreak. Allowing yourself the freedom of acceptance is crucial to the grieving—and consequently the healing—process. When you're able to do this, you'll find yourself becoming stronger and more determined to never again accept any level of abuse or toxicity in your life.

"Your body is a temple of the Holy Spirit within you, which you have from God" (1 Cor. 6:19).

Grief is good. Grief is healing. Grief allows you to move forward with insight, clarity, strength, and a renewed love of self.

Although mourning is difficult and exhausting work, don't hide from the difficulty. Allow the sorrow to wash over you. Feel the grief.

Let it envelop you, but don't let it engulf you. Feel it fully, live it fully, rejoice fully in what it can bring when you reach the other side—but don't let it engulf you within the trickery of despair.

Grieving offers hope, not hopelessness.

The journey from grief to healing takes time. A lot of it. Surround yourself with authentic love as you traverse your path. Find a solid circle of supporting friends and family, an educated spiritual director, a healing support group, or a trusted spiritual community (one that understands abusive situations). Increase your contemplative life through prayer and quiet moments of pure peace. Surround yourself with warmth and self-care.

But, above all else, cry.

Yes, you heard me right. Allow yourself to cry—often and a lot, if need be. Releasing all that pent-up emotion is good not only for the mind, but for your physical body as well.

You're in deep sorrow not only for the death of what you thought you had—and the brutal realization that it was all lies—but the death of your dreams and hopes as well. The precious memories have become intertwined with the traumatic ones, creating a sticky, thorny mixture of disbelief and grief.

Honor that. In the words of St. Catherine of Siena, "it is impossible to reach one's goal without perseverance."[76]

---

[76] St. Catherine of Siena, *The Dialogue,* 52.

Stages of Mourning

Jewel Kilcher, in her excellent autobiography *Never Broken: Songs Are Only Half the Story*, describes her own devastating experience with emotional and psychological abuse at the hands of her mother. "I went through several phases that helped me confront my feelings of betrayal and discovered that each of them had to be experienced fully in order to heal."[77] She then goes on to describe these phases, based on the work of psychotherapist Melanie Brown Kroon. These are:

- Shock.
- Grieving the loss of the betrayer (however that loss may take place).
- Grieving the loss of who you thought that person was.
- Forgiving. During the process of forgiveness, however, there's one crucial thing to remember—the cliché, "forgive and forget" is not only wrong, but ultimately damaging. More on this later.
- Self-forgiveness. This is often the most difficult step because it's more challenging to forgive yourself than it is to forgive others. Most of us tend to be overly self-critical, especially if we still have hurtful words racing through our minds, telling us we're selfish, mean, demanding, stupid, a horrible mother or wife, or any of those other negative accusations we may

---

[77] Jewel Kilcher, *Never Broken: Songs are Only Half the Story* (NY: Blue Rider Press, 2016), 300.

have endured. Jewel has confessed, "shame and humiliation kept me from speaking out for a long time. It has been very, very hard to forgive myself for having been fooled."[78] Sadly, this is a common reaction among abuse victims.

Yet you can successfully work through the shock, the grieving, and the process of forgiveness to reach the ultimate peak of release and healing. Going through the pain of mourning will allow you to gather the strength to embrace life once again, rather than letting it overwhelm you in confusion and despair. Allowing yourself to feel your suffering is the only way to heal from that suffering. Always remember: The most profound and joyous miracle of Jesus' earthly life was the Resurrection—and the Resurrection could never have happened without the excruciating agony of the Crucifixion.

God doesn't rescue us from every tragedy in our lives. That's not how it works in this fallen world. He doesn't rescue us from suffering, but He does walk with us, through the heart of the storm, so we can reach our own personal resurrection. Humanity killed Christ, but God the Father raised Him from the dead. God can do the same for all of us who are suffering from grief, isolation, loneliness, distress, trauma, tragedy, fear and pain—if we allow ourselves to accept the love and Divine Mercy He so desperately wants to give us.

---

[78] Jewel, 302.

Taking the First Steps

Taking the first steps along the healing path can be confusing if you're not sure where to begin. It may seem like an impossible task to heal from such deep trauma, especially as you begin to emerge from your shell and allow yourself to feel the full effects of what was done to you. Be patient with yourself, realizing that healing isn't a linear process. Some days may feel like regression rather than progression, and that's okay—it's all part of the process. Even when you feel like you're rowing against the tide, I promise you that you'll reach the shore.

If needed, go back to chapter four and review the steps to healing that include beginning or maintaining an active prayer life, sharing your story with trusted friends and professionals, keeping a healing journal (as long as you can be assured it won't be found and read by your partner), and listening to your innermost self, that intuitive inner guidance from the Holy Spirit. I also recommend trusted and safe support groups so you can talk to others who are traveling a similar journey—knowing you're not alone, and feeling safe within a circle of friends, can do wonders for healing. Suggestions are provided in the appendix.

Anger

Many people feel stuck because they want to forgive (regardless of whether they want to reconcile), but they still feel angry with the person who hurt them, and perhaps even resentful toward what he's done and how he's controlled their life for so long. They're not sure how to move forward.

The way forward is to recognize those feelings. Embrace them. Love them, even. They're valid.

Anger isn't a bad thing. In fact, it can be quite healthy—as long as it's admitted and processed rather than allowed to turn into contempt and a desire for revenge. Targets of domestic abuse tend to deny anger, believing they're hurt and heartbroken (which they are) but not necessarily angry (which they most often are, and rightfully so). We need to admit this. Anger is good, as long as it's kept in a healthy balance. It's part of the glorious scenery along the path toward healing. The CCC mentions anger as one of the "passions" which "are natural components of the human psyche ... Passions are morally good when they contribute to a good action; evil in the opposite case" (CCC 1764, 1768).

Being angry about the right things and in the right way is virtuous, but avoiding anger at all times may be a sign of weakness. St. Thomas Aquinas states that it's a vice not to get angry over things one should. He calls it "unreasonable patience."[79]

What is the role of anger in forgiveness? How do we use healthy anger to propel us toward self-growth while avoiding the fatal trap of falling into toxic resentment?

It's all about obsession. Those who feel toxic resentment obsess over past hurts and luxuriate in being a victim. This is done for a variety of reasons: because it makes them feel as if they have an

---

[79] Edward Sri, "Anger and Virtue," Catholic Education Resource Center, https://www.catholiceducation.org/en/marriage-and-family/ parenting/anger-and-virtue.html

excuse for their own negative behaviors, because it helps them to avoid feelings of unhealthy shame, because it gains them the attention of other people's empathy. Or, obsessing over past hurts can be a form of dreaming for revenge or "karma" to take its toll on the one who hurt us. None of these attitudes are healthy—and they won't make us into an authentic, whole person. Only the release of forgiveness can do that.

Yet forgiveness doesn't equal reconciliation.

Forgiveness and reconciliation two are completely separate issues, and to confuse them would be detrimental and damaging. Forgiveness also doesn't mean toleration of abusive behavior.

It's also important to realize that forgiveness isn't a one-time event. It's a process, and often a slow one. To force or coerce a false sense of forgiveness because you feel "it's the right thing to do" is actually the wrong thing to do. Instead, acknowledge each emotion as it comes. During the grieving and healing process many emotions will arise, subside, arise again, and swirl together. Take each one as they show up, and honor them all as welcome pieces in the recovery process. Move through your trauma with prayer and self-understanding. Allow forgiveness to eventually flow in a natural, soft way. It will, it just may take time.

And that's perfectly okay. Forgiveness is a skill—which means it takes practice.

The Art of Forgiveness

Forgiveness is the art of giving—of giving to ourselves, to our healing, and to our spiritual growth. It's letting go of anger and resentment and dissolving any desire for revenge or payback. It's a release and a relief.

While forgiveness is not is a memory eraser, nor should it be. "Forgive and forget" is an unhealthy attitude, because it's impossible to forget excruciating trauma, nor should we try. "Forgetting" in this way is merely burying things rather than healing them—or healing *from* them.

As I mentioned before, forgiveness also doesn't mean reconciliation. Just because you forgive doesn't mean you have to share a life with someone who isn't healthy for you. Even after you fully heal, you won't magically forget the trauma you've endured, nor should you. Instead, you'll remember it, acknowledge how you've grown from the suffering you've been through, and recall what the abusive situation was like. This allows you not only to avoid similar situations in the future, but also to feel a healthy sense of much-needed empowerment and self-worth, an acknowledgment of the immense strength it takes to emerge from victim to resilient survivor.

Forgiveness is about release: release of toxic attachment to a situation or person, release of having to dwell on what the person said or did, release to create the space to focus on yourself—on your own God-given strengths and talents, healthy hobbies and pursuits, and the development of close ties with supportive and loving friends and family. The USCCB reminds us that "forgiveness means that the victim decides to let go of the experience and move on with greater insight and conviction not to tolerate abuse of any kind again."[80]

---

[80] USCCB, "When I Call for Help."

Why Bother?

A common question after domestic abuse is why we should bother to forgive. You may feel depleted and broken; you may be angry that he took years away from your life and buried you in pile after pile of deceit, betrayal, and heartbreak. Who deserves for-giveness after that?

When we've been betrayed, controlled, and lied to, we naturally recognize either that a love we once had has been taken from us through manipulative betrayal, or that it never truly existed in the way we thought it had. That hurts. A lot.

After the shock has begun to wear off, feelings of resentment may naturally follow. Yet resentment has a habit of growing, like an internal infection taking over all your bodily organs. At first it's treatable, but if left too long it becomes too pervasive to control. It causes us to obsess over negative situations and possibilities, and it keeps us tied in unhealthy ways to those who have hurt us. Resent-ment tends to spill over into additional areas of our lives, spreading toxicity within our healthy relationships. We become irritable, im-patient, and angry—or exhausted, depressed, and anxious. This cre-ates a ripple effect of isolation and disconnection from others, which makes it difficult to trust anyone, not just the one who actually be-trayed us.

The cure is forgiveness. When we're ready to open ourselves to forgiveness, the path of love will show us how to trust again.

At the earliest stages along the journey of forgiveness, how-ever, the focus on regaining trust isn't on trusting the abuser—some-thing that may never be justified—but rather on learning to trust ourselves again. All of us who have been betrayed by abuse have lost not only the gift of trusting our spouse and by extension others, but of trusting ourselves. That's a tragedy we all need to repair.

The secret rests in charity.

Charity doesn't mean giving your old jeans to Goodwill because you ate too many chocolates, or even donating a few dollars to the collection basket during Sunday Mass. True charity is authentic love; it's a developing of self to the point that self merges with the goodness of others, of allowing oneself to be vulnerable enough to enjoy true fellowship and relationship, to recognize the image and likeness of God within others, no matter how different they may be from us. True charity is loving the other for the sake of their beautiful selves, and not for the sake of our own egoistic needs. True charity is also the ability to give freely in order to accept freely. It's the ability to fully receive God as He appears through the gifts of humanity.

True charity is love of others, which begins with love of self. And loving self is the definition of authentic healing.

I understand. I've been there. Processing my own grief, and the subsequent loss of connection with self and others, has led to a slow awakening. As the healing began, I shivered with the pain of the process. It hurt. A lot. But I made it through, and I made it through with love; love of self, love of God, and a renewed trust in others. I know that without charity, I'm nothing more than a noisy gong or a clanging cymbal.

And who wants to be that?

God the Father told St. Catherine of Siena in a mystical vision: "The soul cannot live without love. She always wants to love something, because she is made of love, and through love I created her."

We've been made for love. That's how our Father designed us, and how He designed us to heal.

Above all else, remember that you're a survivor. "All things are possible to those who believe" (Mark 9:23). *All* things are possible—even healing from domestic abuse and regaining the ability to develop strong, healthy, reliable and authentic relationships with others.

Beginning with yourself.

And God.

"For I know the plans I have for you, says the LORD, plans for welfare and not for evil, to give you a future and a hope" (Jer. 29:11).

Appendix A

An Abuse Dictionary

(an excerpt from my Substack blog, https://www.createsoulspace.org)

This section is by no means complete—there are a myriad of abuse terms I could mention, but the goal here is to describe the most common.

An Abuse Dictionary

Abuse Cycle — The abuse cycle is a four-stage pattern of behavior that can be seen in many (but not all) abusive relationships. These four stages of the cycle of abuse are generally known as tension, incident, reconciliation, calm. However, some experts use different terms (for example, "honeymoon" instead of "reconciliation").

Not all abusive relationships are cyclical, so the four-stage cycle of abuse isn't accurate for everyone. Even so, it's true in many toxic interactions, and it helps identify how the pattern of abuse can play out in some relationships. Keep in mind, though, that the cycle of abuse doesn't take into account the individuality of each person or relationship, or how a victim might experience abuse from their partner.

Baiting — If you're with someone who uses abusive tactics as a means of manipulating and controlling your relationship, you may have experienced "baiting." This is when your partner provokes a strong reaction from you, pushing you beyond your limits until you respond in an angry or desperate manner.

Once you've taken the "bait" and reacted strongly, your partner has created a way to retaliate. You may be accused of being the abuser in the relationship, or told that you're crazy and unhinged.

You're none of those things! It's important to renounce those lies. For example, you can pray, "In the name of Jesus, I renounce the lie that I'm crazy. In the name of Jesus, I take back the truth that I'm strong and I have my own God-given mind."

Belittling — Pretending verbal abuse is "just a joke" and that sarcasm is acceptable is another distinct and damaging form of abuse. "Just a joke" and sarcasm are both covert attacks at your very personhood and are demeaning to your dignity as a person made in the image and likeness of God.

Breadcrumbing — Breadcrumbing occurs when an abusive individual drops small crumbs of tenderness, warmth, or positive attention into their relationship. The goal is that of keeping you hooked with the delusion that love and mutual affection can actually exist between the two of you.

This type of emotional abuse habituates you into tolerating toxic behavior—all with your perpetual hope of receiving some crumbs of love from time to time.

Cognitive Dissonance — Cognitive dissonance describes the excruciating confusion of trying to grasp two contradictory beliefs at the same time. For example, it's likely very difficult to reconcile the "Dr. Jekyll" part of your partner with their "Mr. Hyde" part.

Cognitive dissonance is particularly distressing when we intuitively know the truth, yet we doubt our own reality (see "Gaslighting"). What we see at any given time isn't necessarily what we get—and this is so painfully confusing.

Countering — The person in your life who is using abuse to control you opposes everything you express or try to communicate to them—even if it's your own opinion or you have irrefutable proof of what you're attempting to tell them. The abuser often says the same thing you were saying, then denies you were saying it and claims the opposite. This is crazy-making at it's best!

It can be easy to confuse countering with simple disagreement, but there are crucial differences. People don't always see eye-to-eye—differences of opinion are normal and even healthy when expressed in a constructive manner. However, countering is never healthy because the one countering tends to be irrational and hypocritical in what they say, with an underlying resentment and anger simply due to the fact that you're expressing your own individual beliefs, thoughts, feelings, and opinions. When you hold fast to your own point of view, someone with an abusive part feels their control slipping away. They want to be the one to tell you what you believe and hold to be true. In other words, they want to control all aspects of your life—including your own thoughts.

Crazy-Making — Have you ever been told that you're crazy, that maybe something is wrong with your head (whether psychologically or medically), that you're losing you're grip on reality? Perhaps you feel you are. Yet deep down, your gut intuition says *no!* Your perceptions are real, even if they are being constantly denied and countered (see above). Well, that's crazy-making at its best. If you doubt yourself, your beliefs and preferences, if you can't seem to do things on your own any longer, crazy-making may be at play. Crazy-making includes denial of things the abuser has done, claimed, or statements they've made in the past; twisting situations to place responsibility onto you in an attempt to prove your mental instability or sketchy memory; and outright lying to further convince you of how crazy you are.

DARVO — Deny—Attack—Reverse Victim and Offender. DARVO an acronym for a series of manipulative tactics that a perpetrator will use to deny their wrongdoing by attacking the person they offended, then reversing the roles and trying to make themselves out to be a victim when in fact they're the offender.

This powerful form of manipulation twists the focus away from whatever problem the true victim may have tried to bring up, thus enabling the perpetrator to completely avoid the issue as well as all accountability for abusive behaviors.

The DARVO tactic of manipulation generally plays out like this:

- **Deny.** The perpetrator intensely denies whatever concern the true victim is wanting to talk about. This form of gaslighting involves a twisting or reality in an effort to "get off the hook" and cause the target of the manipulation doubt their perception or memory of events, or even their own reality. The target often wonders if they're "blowing things out of proportion" or "being too sensitive"—as the abuser claims. For example, perhaps the target found incriminating text messages of a sexual nature on her partner's phone, so she confronts him about infidelity. He counters with a denial that the texts weren't sexual in nature, claiming she "read them wrong."

- **Attack**. The perpetrator twists the focus of the conversation, goes on the defensive and acts shocked to be "accused" of something which they did, in fact, do. For example, the perpetrator could attack by saying, "What were you doing snooping on my phone? You're so controlling and ridiculous. I can't believe you even did that! What's wrong with you?" Which then sets the stage for ....

- **Reverse Victim and Offender.** The ultimate phase of the twisted tactic of DARVO is for the perpetrator insist they're the "victim" in the situation, that they're the one being abused and that they're owed a groveling apology. They'll then use their so-called "victimhood status" as a way to further abuse and manipulate their target into compliance—and they'll also hold the situation against their partner in the future, at any time it suits them best. For example, "You always control me, and mistrust me. I can't do anything right in this relationship. I try so hard, but you still doubt me. There's no way I can please you, even though I try. Still, I love you and will put up with you because that's just the type of person I am …"

Flying Monkeys — This is the term used to describe individuals who—knowingly or unknowingly—collaborate with an abuser in carrying out manipulative tactics. Named after the submissive slaves of the Wicked Witch of the West in the Wizard of Oz, flying monkeys seem to be held under the spell of an abuser, and do his or her bidding without question.

It can be very difficult to identify a flying monkey since they may seem to be caring people who merely take sides in a certain conflict or relationship. Often, they don't understand that they're being manipulated by a controlling personality. Instead, they faithfully assist the abuser by attacking the victim in whatever way they're told—because they've been brainwashed to do so.

This common abusive tactic uses family, friends, and even members of your local community to spread lies and gossip about you, to spy on you, and to otherwise make you out to be the perpetrator.

Gaslighting — This tactic encompasses so much. For example, crazy-making, countering, denial … these are all forms of gaslighting.

Gaslighting happens when a person uses subtle ways to condition and convince his or her target that their own reality, feelings and beliefs are inaccurate. Typically, a gaslighter uses various covert tactics in order to consciously or even unconsciously brainwash their victim. For example, they might deny saying or doing something that they obviously said or did, or they might convince you that you heard wrong or that your memory is faulty.

If you're a victim of gaslighting, you may doubt yourself and even your own sanity, which leads to greater dependence upon others—especially upon the person who is gaslighting you. You find yourself turning to them to define your reality, because you no longer feel strong enough to trust your own perceptions.

Hoovering — (see below, "Love bombing") Once the relationship has been established and the toxic part of the individual shows up, the abuse cycle begins in earnest. After an abusive incident escalates, the person with narcissistic traits may afterward act contrite and begin another round of flattery, gifts, being extra kind, etc. This stage of the abuse cycle is designed to suck you back into the web of the relationship and is called "hoovering," named after the Hoover vacuum cleaner.

Love Bombing — This is the phrase used to describe what typically happens in the initial stage of a relationship with someone who has a strong abuse part to their personality. A form of psychological and emotional abuse, love bombing happens when the manipulating individual goes out of their way to impress you by flattering you, buying you wonderful gifts, painting an amazing future for the two of them, telling you "I've never felt this way about anyone before," and doing other things to make you feel as if they've met their soul mate.

Projection — Also known as blame-shifting, this tactic was first described by Anna Freud in 1936 when she recognized a self-defense mechanism that people use in order to avoid unwanted feelings about themselves, or to shift their negative thoughts and behaviors onto others. Chances are most of us have done this from time to time, but a major red flag starts waving when the tactic becomes a recurrent and unrelenting pattern in a relationship.

This form of manipulation becomes toxic when a person frequently shifts responsibility for something negative they've done— or for the personality flaws they have—in order blame their target for being the "bad guy." For example, if they're a neglectful parent, they'll blame their spouse for being neglectful, even though the opposite is true. They refuse to admit any wrongdoing, instead blaming others for the specific thing that they're guilty of. This helps them to both avoid shame and to feel superior.

Trauma Bond — A trauma bond is when a victim forms a powerful, fiercely faithful emotional tie with their abuser, even though they're enduring the suffering of cyclical and toxic mistreatment.

Although it may not feel like it, this is a psychological and also chemical bond, not an emotional one. It's the cyclical nature of the abuse—one moment he's Dr. Jekyll, bringing roses and gushing love (see "hoovering" and "love bombing"), and the next Mr. Hyde appears, spewing all sorts of verbal, emotional, perhaps even physical venom. From a psychological point of view, this is what forms a trauma bond (see "breadcrumbing"). Yet more is at play here. Our brain releases chemicals when we're stressed, anxious, under threat … As well as when those feelings are relieved. When they're relieved, we crave more of that brain chemical in order to feel safe. This is why the "good times" in a toxic relationship feel so very, very good. They ease the bursting pressure. They provide relief.

Triangulation — Triangulation describes a form of manipulation in which an individual tries to control an intimate situation by bringing in a third party, with the goal of attempting to verify or coerce their point of view.

This tactic is all about twisting a situation to create conflict and/or miscommunication. As with all other abusive tactics, this may or may not be intentional on the part of the manipulator—yet that doesn't matter. The end result is the same, and it's still abuse.

Some individuals with abusive tendencies use the manipulative tactic of triangulation as yet another way to seek control over their partners. In this tactic, abusers manipulate their victim by talking with a person outside of their relationship about intimate (and often false) details regarding their partner. They target someone who is close to their partner—a friend, family member, a co-worker, etc.—in order to create conflict and miscommunication. The goal is to make the abuser look like the "good guy," because they can then be the mediator of the situation or appear to be the one source of stability.

Trivializing — Trivializing is a demeaning tactic that minimizes, ignores, or otherwise downplays of your life, beliefs, career, efforts to repair the relationship (or any other effort you put forth), your interests, emotions, or your worries. This is a covert method of abuse, often hidden under an innocent-seeming shroud of "I just care for you …"

Examples of trivializing include:

- "It's great that you earned your master's degree in visual art! But what can you even do with that degree, except teach? I only ask because I care about you and want what's best for your future."
- "I come home from work, and the house is so messy. What have you been doing all day?" (When, in reality, you've been homeschooling the kids, doing the laundry and dishes, changing diapers and … well, the list can go on and varies from person to person, but you get the idea.)
- "You like to write short stories? That's a great hobby. I've never been interested in fiction myself, though. I'm so busy with my career, I don't have that sort of leisure time to waste."

Withholding — A form of emotional abuse in which the person who is acting abusively withholds affection, conversation, mutual self-giving, emotional support, or physical attention. Refusing to effectively or actively communicate is another form of withholding, and one that can be particularly confusing to the victim.

If you've a victim of withholding, you may feel ignored, lonely, isolated, or as if your life isn't your own because you have no control over what's happening. Confusion sets in and takes root in the mind, particularly because withholding is most often alternated with hoovering, thereby creating a solid trauma bond.

Word salad — This is when a manipulator craftily spins words into a confusing jumble to confuse their target so thoroughly that out of sheer exhaustion the target decides to believe whatever is being said.

After all, it's easier that way. Interestingly, this phrase originally came from the field of psychiatry, where it's often used to describe the speech of those who suffer from mental health conditions such as schizophrenia.

In a situation when the tactic of word salad is at play, the conversation goes nowhere despite all your efforts otherwise. You try—and try, and try again—to explain your thoughts, feelings, etc., but all you get is a jumbled, convoluted response that folds words in on themselves, or scrambles them up into non-comprehension. What your partner is saying—and how they're responding—makes no sense, despite the fact that you're being so careful to communicate properly. Even so, you're getting confusion in response, and blame that you're the one with the communication problem.

If you'd like a PDF of some of these abuse terms, please contact me at https://jennydubay.com/contact-me/ and I can email it to you.

Appendix B

Are You in an Abusive Marriage?
Here are 30 Warning Signs

(an excerpt from my Substack blog, https://www.createsoulspace.org)

There are many red flags and warning signs that indicate you may be in an abusive marriage, but, unfortunately, they're easy to miss unless a person is familiar with the tactics and traits of domestic abusers. Many signs of potential abuse are extremely covert and disguised as devotion or caring, such as possessive jealousy in the guise of "it's because I love you so much," or "I've never felt this way about anyone before." Other signs are baffling due to gaslighting and circular talk, causing a target's head to swim with confusion. You may believe him when he claims the two of you merely have a "communication problem," or you may suffer from a depleted sense of self-worth because you think all the issues in your relationship are entirely (or mainly) your fault.

Recognizing the warning signs of abuse is the crucial first step toward healing and regaining your sense of self. When you realize you're in an abusive marriage, you can then take steps to educate yourself, make a necessary safety plan, seek outside support, and even find professional help.

Remember that *abuse is a habitual pattern.* When someone consistently hurts, demeans, betrays, or criticizes another, it's abuse. If your partner has engaged in behaviors once or twice during your relationship, and authentically apologized without repeating the same behavior again and again, that isn't chronic abuse. That's being human, making mistakes, and making amends. However, if any of these behaviors are engaged in "often" or "occasionally," you're likely noticing a pattern.

Rate each statement with "often," "occasionally," "rarely," or "never."

- You've forgotten yourself—things you used to enjoy no longer interest you, your social life is on the decline, you've lost touch with friends and family, or you simply don't feel like yourself any longer.
- When you share things with him, particularly of a very personal or deep nature, they're eventually used against you. You may even have given up sharing anything about yourself, for fear of retaliation.
- You experience fear, anxiety, or confusion when you're around your partner.
- You put your partner's needs above your own, all the time—because you're afraid to express your own needs, even to yourself.
- Your spouse demeans, belittles, or mocks you, or treats you like a child instead of an equal partner.
- You wonder if you're crazy or if there's something wrong with you, because the way you remember a certain event, argument, or issue is vastly different from how he remembers it.

- You avoid doing certain things, going out with friends, dressing the way you prefer, or going on social media because you're afraid of making your partner angry.
- It feels like you can't say anything right, because he twists your words and convinces himself that you have bad intentions or are deliberately trying to hurt him.
- Your spouse nearly always blames you when things go wrong in your relationship, regardless of the situation or circumstance—and isn't open to hearing your side of the situation.
- You feel too ashamed to tell anyone what's going on behind the closed doors of your home, or feel that if you were honest with a friend, you'd be betraying your spouse.
- Your finances are controlled by your partner, and you don't have much say in how money is spent, invested, or saved.
- Unrealistic expectations or demands are placed on you, and anger is sure to follow if you don't comply.
- Your spouse often yells, slams doors, or makes other gestures of rage and potential violence.
- When your partner gets angry he's prone to throwing things and destroying property—but, if you think about it, it's only your property he destroys, not his own.
- Even though you're in a committed relationship, you feel deeply alone and without a friend to confide in.
- Your spouse denies things he said or did, causing you to feel as if you're going crazy and making you doubt your own memories and sense of reality.
- Your partner calls you names or makes you feel stupid/worthless in other ways.

- He makes threats when he gets upset—such as threats of leaving you, taking the children, killing himself, hurting you or your pets, withdrawing financial support, etc.

- If you voice a difference of opinion or don't agree with something your spouse says or does, there's a hefty price to pay.

- You feel obligated to have sex with him, even when you don't want to.

- You feel like you're walking on eggshells or can't be yourself within what should be the comfort of your own home.

- Your partner has a "Dr. Jekyll/Mr. Hyde" personality. One day (or minute) he can be charming, sweet, sensitive, and caring, and then next he turns into someone you never imagined—someone scary.

- You're constantly second-guessing yourself, worried you said or did the wrong thing and afraid your spouse will get upset or angry at you.

- When you're not together, your partner calls or texts often, checking up on where you are or what you're doing. Sometimes he claims it's "just to say hi," but the communications are unusually frequent throughout the day.

- He accuses you of doing things you didn't do—such as cheating on him or flirting with other men.

- Your partner has physically injured you or has threatened to injure you.

- He claims you're incapable of living without him or wouldn't survive without his care.

- If you apologize for something you did—no matter how small—one apology isn't enough; you have to grovel, apologize over and over, before he'll let the issue drop (but then, even years later, the issue will inevitably resurface, and he'll forget that you ever apologized in the first place). Or, you're forced to apologize for things you never did (including things he's guilty of doing).

- He consistently denies your needs, yet he demands 24/7 attention from you.
- Drugs or alcohol are used as an excuse for toxic and abusive behavior, including cruel name-calling or acts of violence.

Sadly, this is a very brief and abbreviated summary of behaviors. There are many other signs of abuse I could mention, but the list would be too long. However, you now have a starting point, and things to consider. If you answered "often" or "occasionally" to any of these statements, you may be in an abusive relationship. If you answered "often" or "occasionally" to several of these statements, please seek help and healing, and educate yourself about intimate partner violence.

Keep in mind that individuals who use abuse to control and manipulate others are experts. They can be very cunning, crafty, covert, and sly—so it can be difficult to recognize abuse when it's present in a relationship. The more you read, the more you learn, the more you pray and seek help, the stronger you'll become in fighting this malignant relationship destroyer.

Appendix C

Finding Support

The National Domestic Violence Hotline:
https://www.thehotline.org or call 800-799-SAFE (7233)

Search for local help: https://www.domesticshelters.org/help

Create Soul Space, helping Catholics heal from domestic abuse: https://www.createsoulspace.net

Jenny duBay, Trauma-Informed Catholic Life Coach specializing in domestic abuse and betrayal trauma: https://jennydubay.com

Hope's Garden, a Catholic women's community including a safe and interactive forum for betrayal trauma and domestic abuse, prayer groups, coaching, courses, podcast, and more: https://hopesgarden.com

Hope's Garden Domestic Violence Support Groups: https://hopesgarden.com/domestic-violence-resources/

The CHRIST Program through Hope's Garden is a complete program teaching Christ-centered therapeutic skills to help you discover the right balance between acceptance and change: accepting that which is outside of your control, while practicing therapeutic skills to help you make important changes in your thoughts, emotions and behaviors.

https://hopesgarden.com/christ-program-subscription/

For more healing courses, see
https://jennydubay.com/courses-through-hopes-garden/

You Are Made New Ministry, healing through the integration of therapeutic practices and our Catholic faith:
https://youaremadenew.com

Catholics for Family Peace: A Catholic Response to Domestic Abuse and Violence: http://www.catholicsforfamilypeace.org

Free eBook from Dr. Christauria Welland, *How Can We Help End Violence in Catholic Families: A Guide for Clergy, Religious and Laity*: http://paxinfamilia.org/wp-content/uploads/2019/07/How-can-we-help-to-end-violence-2nd-edition.pdf

Domestic Violence Outreach from the Archdiocese of Chicago: https://pvm.archchicago.org/human-dignity-solidarity/domestic-violence-outreach

Catholic Charities: https://www.catholiccharitiesusa.org

USCCB, "When I Call for Help": https://www.usccb.org/topics/marriage-and-family-life-ministries/when-i-call-help-pastoral-response-domestic-violence

Educational Resources:

For a thorough list of books, articles, YouTube videos and podcasts on all aspects of domestic abuse, visit https://www.createsoul-space.net/narcissistic-abuse-resources.html

A self-paced course to educate clergy and laity working within various parish ministries, Dr. Christauria Welland's course *Violence & Abuse in Catholic and Christian Families: Preparing an Effective and Compassionate Pastoral Response* is highly recommended: https://health-transformations.learnworlds.com/course/violence-and-abuse-in-catholic-and-christian-families

Internal Family Systems (IFS):

I highly recommend Dr. Gerry Crete's book, *Litanies of the Heart: Relieving Post-Traumatic Stress and Calming Anxiety Through Healing Our Parts.* https://sophiainstitute.com/product/litanies-of-the-heart/

I also recommend *Altogether You: Experiencing Personal and Spiritual Transformation with Internal Family Systems Therapy* by Jenna Riemersma, LPC. https://jennariemersma.com/book/

Dr. Peter Malinoski hosts an IFS-based podcast called *Interior Integration for Catholics* (https://www.soulsandhearts.com/iic/)

Find a Catholic IFS therapist at: https://www.soulsandhearts.com/therapists/

Declaration of Nullity:

For brief information and a list of resources, visit https://www.createsoulspace.net/all-about-annulment.html.

From the USCCB: https://www.usccb.org/topics/marriage-and-family-life-ministries/annulment#tab--what-is-an-annulment

Catholic Annulment FAQs: https://togetherforlifeonline.com/catholic-annulment/ and https://www.foryourmarriage.org/annulments/.

Appendix D

Creating a Safety Plan
(from DomesticShelters.org)

Creating a safety plan is crucial for anyone in an abusive situation, regardless of whether you've ever been physically harmed. Remember that violent and toxic behaviors escalate the longer they continue, and emotional abuse often moves into the realm of physical abuse. Even if your situation never turns physical, a safety plan is essential.

However, a safety plan isn't a substitute for dialing 911 if you need immediate help. Never hesitate to get the assistance you need, when you need it, from safe and supportive people.

Creating a safety plan with a professional is ideal. To find help in your area, you can call the Domestic Violence Hotline at 800-799-7233. If it's safe for you, you could put this number in your phone for quick dialing—but put it under a random name (for example, "Alice," so it appears at the top of your contact list for easy access), something you can readily find but no one will suspect. Again—and I can't stress this enough—only do this if it's completely safe for you. Your safety must always come first.

If you don't have professional resources available, you can still create your own safety plan. This doesn't have to mean you're going to permanently leave the relationship. For some survivors, permanently leaving may be the best option—but for others, it may be dangerous, unwanted or unfeasible for a variety of reasons. Everyone's situation is different—trust your instincts and, above all, *pray constantly.* Even if you never end up using it, having a solid plan in place can bring tremendous peace of mind.

What a safety plan can do for you is to help you escape a terrifying incident with your abuser—whether that escape happens in the moment (if that's safe for you) or in the aftermath. Once you're safe, you can—with the help and support of others—clear your head and heart enough to figure out what you want to do next.

In the heat of an abusive incident, if it's not safe to leave the situation, you can still take precautions. Move to a room that provides you with a means of escape should that become necessary, a place with a door or window you can easily access. Don't seek refuge in a closed-in-area, such as a bathroom or walk-in closet, or in a room with potential weapons, such as a kitchen.

Use your God-given instincts—and trust them. Believe your gut feelings, even if your mind tries to debunk what your instincts are shouting at you. Stay safe.

"Cast all your anxieties on God, for He cares about you. Be sober, be watchful … After you have suffered a little while the God of all grace will Himself restore, establish, and strengthen you" (1 Pet. 5:7,10).

DomesticShelters.org has a wealth of information on all aspects of domestic violence, including how to create a safety plan and how to customize your plan. With their generous permission, I'm reprinting their articles to help you better understand what a safety plan is, and how to create one for yourself.[81]

A Safety Planning Worksheet

A safety plan can increase the chances you a.) escape a threatening, scary or violent encounter with an abuser safely, even if it's a temporary escape and b.) help you solidify a plan to leave an abuser permanently, prepared with what you need to file charges if you so choose and start a new life over without having to contact the abuser again.

A safety plan does not mean you need to leave your home forever. In the plan, you will think about where you can go temporarily to be safe and consider next steps. Those next steps may be acquiring an order of protection that forces the abuser to leave your home, breaking a lease or initiating divorce proceedings. For some survivors, leaving a home they share with an abuser for good turns out to be the safest option, but remember, it's all up to you and what you deem safest and doable.

What a Safety Plan is NOT

---

[81] I give great thanks to the wonderful staff at Domestic Shelters, who gave me permission to use their safety planning information in this book. Domesticshelters.org, "Safety Planning Worksheet," https://www.domesticshelters.org/articles/safety-planning/a-safety-planning-worksheet; "Customizing your safety plan," https://www.domesticshelters.org/articles/safety-planning/ customizing-your-safety-plan.

A safety plan is not a replacement for calling 911, filing an order of protection or contacting a lawyer. In many cases, a safety plan involves some of those steps.

Step 1: Prepare

- **Collect evidence.** If it is safe to do so, keeping a journal of abusive incidents (date, time, details), including threats, as well as copies of threatening or abusive emails, text messages, police reports, doctor or hospital records will be helpful if and when you file for an order of protection or press charges against an abuser. Keep this evidence outside of your home, like at a workplace, a friend's house or a safety deposit box.

I can keep the evidence I've collected or will collect, which includes:

- _____

- _____

- _____

- _____

at _____ (safe place the abuser won't find).

- **Stash a getaway bag.** This bag, which you should, again, keep somewhere where the abuser can't find it, such as a friend's house, your workplace or a neighbor's house, will contain important documents such as: your driver's license, passport, birth certificate, social security cards, copies of financial records, your lease or deed, health insurance information, prescriptions, marriage license or divorce papers, and all similar paperwork for your children, if applicable. It should also include, if possible, some cash you are able to save in case the abuser cancels credits cards or blocks you from accessing bank accounts.

I will make sure to pack the following in my getaway bag:

- _____
- _____
- _____
- _____

and will hide it at _____ *(safe place the abuser won't find).*

Step 2: Plan

- **Decide where to go.** When it's time to leave—it could be while the abuser is at work, the next time you feel in danger, exactly two weeks from now or whenever you deem the best time—you need to plan where to go. Consider an emergency shelter (which will need advance notice, so contact an advocate there), a friend or family member's house that the abuser doesn't know the location of or is far enough away that it will be difficult for the abuser to get to you, or, if affordable, a hotel or apartment that you pay for with cash so the abuser cannot track you there. Keep in mind that if you have a cell phone, the abuser may be able to trace your location, so consider getting a pay-as-you-go temporary phone and leaving your cell behind.

I will be leaving _____ *(approximate date/time) and going to* _____. *I will only tell* _____*(trusted friend/family member/advocate) of my whereabouts.*

- **Plan for all possibilities.** You know your partner best. You know what abusive tactics he or she is most likely to use. Make sure you think about that as you get ready to leave. The abuser may feel like something is different in your demeanor and may become more controlling. When an abuser feels like they are losing control, it is often the most dangerous time for a survivor. Prepare for this by thinking out different scenarios that could happen and what you will do. For example, if an abuser always shuts the bedroom door to close you in before he or she becomes violent, can you unlock a window ahead of time, given you're on the ground floor, and exit through it when this starts? If an abuser threatens to keep or harm your children or pets if you leave, can you make sure they're in a safe place before you leave, such as taking them to a trusted relative's house? Can you create a code word that, if you say it in front of your children, they'll know to run next door to the neighbor's house and call 911?

I know my partner is likely to use the following tactics to control me and keep me from leaving:

- _____
- _____
- _____
- _____

To counteract these things, I will prepare by doing the following:

- _____
- _____
- _____
- _____

Step 3: After You Leave

- **Stay vigilant.** After you leave an abuser, or after an abuser is forced to leave your home, you'll want to take safety precautions to keep yourself and your family safe. This should include considering an order of protection, alerting your place of employment and your children's school what is going on and giving them a photo of the abuser so they can alert you if he or she comes around, using a different route to get to and from work or school, changing your schedule, taking a break from social media so the abuser is less likely to track or harass you, and changing your phone number and making it unlisted.

After I leave, I will do the following actions to help keep myself safe:

- _____
- _____
- _____
- _____
- _____

This is a basic plan to leave an abuser, but there are many things to consider when doing so. If children or pets are involved, special considerations need to be made, so extra research and planning is required. The more you know, the better.

Customizing Your Safety Plan

Creating a safety plan is a vital step when one is considering leaving an abusive partner. In doing so, this plan can help a survivor strategize what they will do to stay safe—and keep their children and pets safe—in the midst of abuse, be it to escape temporarily during an incidence of violence or when they're ready to leave their abuser for good.

Leaving an abusive partner is notoriously the most dangerous time for a survivor. As an abuser feels they are losing power over their victim, they can become increasingly more controlling, threatening, violent or may even turn lethal.

Below, three steps to follow when you're ready to create your own safety plan.

Step 1: Abate Your Fears

Some survivors of domestic violence are rightly fearful that implementing the steps in a safety plan will place them more at risk with their abuser. After all, packing a bag or trying to find copies of important paperwork could raise suspicions with your abuser. Survivors are wise to know that this can be a very volatile time, says Marylouise Kelley, director, Division of Family Violence Prevention and Service, whose office supports domestic violence shelters nationwide, through funding, awareness, and support. "The survivor is the expert on her own life. She has the best sense of how dangerous her situation is."

As such, consider an order of protection as part of your safety planning. When you're ready to leave, your abuser can be served with this order simultaneously, creating a legal disincentive for him or her from making contact with you while you find safety. A domestic violence advocate in your area can help you secure an order of protection.

Regardless of where you're at in the leaving process, Kelley says planning ahead is still helpful. "I think it's really important to gather information, even if you're not ready to make a move. [A survivor] can reach out to a local program and ask questions about what their options are, without ever having to disclose to someone that they've done that."

Plus, she adds, "If you're in the midst of a crisis it's really hard to think straight. Putting a plan in place ahead of time, knowing where things are and having children understand what steps they can take to be safe—those are all things that are best done in advance."

Step 2: Find Your Advocate

You can read all about safety planning, but since your abuser is different than someone else's abuser, and since you know him or her better than anyone, your safety plan will need to be customized to fit your unique scenario. You know what time of day will be safest to leave, a place you can go where he or she won't be able to find you and what steps you need to put in place beforehand—such as acquiring an order of protection or making sure your child's school is aware of the situation—in order to ensure safety after you leave.

But in the midst of such stress, it can help to not go at this alone. A trained domestic violence advocate can help you sort through everything you need to do and plan for in order to create a safety plan that makes the most sense, something that Kelley recommends as well.

"It is the critical role of an advocate to talk to a survivor about safety planning. When we ask survivors what they need, the number one thing they ask for is an opportunity to talk about their options … and how they can go about [leaving] safely."

Step 3: Plan for All Possibilities

Safety plans need take into consideration all aspects a survivor is dealing with, says Kelley. "Consider who is involved, what family members are affected." Below, some different variations of safety planning to consider:

- **Children**: If there are children in the home, safety plan with them. The National Domestic Violence Hotline offers up safety plan tips when children are involved. You can reach them by calling 800-700-SAFE. Some tips including teaching children never to intervene during a violent incident, and make up a code word you can use when they need to leave the home because of violence.
- **Pets:** You may want to establish custody of your pets before leaving, and make a solid list of what to pack in your safety kit so you can take care of your furry friends.
- **Teens/College Students:** LoveisRespect.org has created comprehensive safety plans both for teens and for college students who are currently dealing with an abusive partner.
- **Pre-Packing**: Finally, when packing a bag, consider including some or most of the essential advocates say you may need once you leave, such as your credit cards,

passport/license, birth certificate, precious keepsakes, toys for your children, personal journal or other records of abuse, and a prepaid cell phone or a cell phone with a new number. It's important you keep this bag in a place where your abuser wouldn't look for it, such as at a friend or neighbor's home, or at your place of work.

Appendix E

Prayers to St. Dymphna and St. Paul

Prayer for the Intercession of St. Dymphna

St. Dymphna, you understand my suffering. You were abused by the one closest to you, within your own home. You know the fear, loss of safety, confusion, and betrayal caused by the harmful behavior of the one you trust and love. Please intercede for me now. Help me to be open to God's grace and His safety plan for me. Pray that, like you, I will be able to create firm boundaries in order to honor and protect God's precious gift of my dignity as the Father's beloved daughter and Jesus' pure bride. I ask all this in the most Precious Name of Jesus. Amen.

A Repentant Soul's Prayer to Saint Paul

St. Paul, I need your intercession. I want to walk the Road to Damascus with you. On this journey, our Lord and Savior changed the entire course of your life. You were an abusive man, persecuting Christ's beloved followers, but He shook the scales from your eyes and revealed His truth to you. I ask Him to change the course of my life beginning today.

I understand now that when I violate the dignity of others, especially those whom God has entrusted to my care, I violate Christ Himself.

In His mercy, may He remove the scales from my eyes. May He heal me, reveal His truth to me, and shower me with His Divine Mercy.

Through the cleansing Blood of Christ and His most Merciful Heart, I pray for your help and guidance, St. Paul, as I travel my own Road to Damascus. May I become the whole, healed, and authentically loving man, husband, father, and child of God I was created to be. In Jesus' name I pray. Amen.

(prayers written by Jenny duBay and Laura Ercolino of Hope's Garden)

Appendix F

A Daughter's Poem of Love:
Soaring After Domestic Abuse

Domestic violence is insidious, evil, and destructive to everyone in its path. Even if a child is not being directly mistreated, if he or she lives in an abusive household where their mother is the target, the psychological and emotional effects are still enormous. Although an abuser may carefully control his actions so the children supposedly don't see or know, they do. They can sense things, feel things, observe things—especially changes in their beloved mother. And this hurts them. A lot.

That is one of my deepest sorrows. Yet at the same time, my (now adult) children have been of utmost comfort, and have tremendously supported me during the healing process. They are always there for me, always showing their love and faith in me.

My daughter has gifted me with a gorgeous poem of healing and grace, and I want to share it with everyone. I hope all survivors of domestic abuse can see how this poem applies to them, as well.

A Daughter's Poem of Love: Soaring After Domestic Abuse
by Keariel Peasley

Your wings were blue,
Like the heavens, like the sea, like melancholy,
They knew instinctively that flight was their fate, were created
solely to soar,

241

That they guided you to flowers, that the nectar was sweet,
That your realm was limitless; you could reach any height.

Your wings were blue, a most royal blue,
Painted by God and passed down through Grammy,
For no lineage is superior
To that of Love.

Your wings were still blue,
Even when they were clipped,
Rendering sweet flowers too high and the sky an impossibility.
Their blueness remained even when folded behind you,
Where you couldn't see them, forgot they were there,
Their presence seemed a dim memory,
When you crawled on the ground, thought you'd get nowhere,
But I saw your wings, brilliant blue tucked away,
And I knew that with enough faith and strength,
You'd recall their presence, unfurl them,
To match the vibrance of the celestial sphere,
To feel the wind carry you, to taste the sweetest flowers again,
For wings serve only one purpose:

to fly.

So, my dear, your wings are still blue,
And I see them still now,
As blue as God painted and Grammy gifted,
As blue as my eyes that know their splendor,

And know that a butterfly lives to soar; let the wind be your guide
and the flowers revive you,
As you open your wings in the sun and they shimmer
In their brilliant hue.
For no matter how long they've been hidden,
Your wings will always be there.

AND THEY WILL ALWAYS BE BLUE.

Bibliography

Arabi, Shahida. "Intermittent Reinforcement: The Powerful Manipulation Method that Keeps You Trauma Bonded to Your Abuser." Thought Catalog, https://thoughtcatalog.com/shahida-arabi/2017/11/this-powerful-manipulation-method-keeps-you-bonded-to-your-abuser/

Arabi, Shahida. *Becoming the Narcissist's Nightmare: How do Devalue and Discard the Narcissist While Supplying Yourself.* NY, NY: SCW Archer Publishing, 2016.

Arabi, Shahida. *Power: Surviving & Thriving After Narcissistic Abuse.* Brooklyn, NY: Thought Catalog Books, 2017.

Bancroft, Lundy. *Why Does He Do That? Inside the Minds of Angry and Controlling Men.* NY, NY: Berkley Books, 2002.

Bancroft, Lundy. *Daily Wisdom for Why Does He Do That? Encouragement for Women Involved with Angry and Controlling Men.* NY, NY: Berkley Books, Penguin Group, 2015.

Bancroft, Lundy and Jac Patrissi. *Should I Stay or Should I Go? A Guide to Knowing if Your Relationship Can—and Should—Be Saved.* NY, NY: Berkley Books, 2001.

Behary, Wendy T., LCSW. *Disarming the Narcissist, Second Edition: Surviving & Thriving with the Self-Absorbed.* Oakland, CA: New Harbinger Publications, Inc., 2013.

Bergsma, John and Brant Pitre. *A Catholic Introduction to the Bible, Volume I: The Old Testament.* San Francisco, CA: Ignatius Press, 2018.

Bois, Paul. "Pornhub Under Fire After Videos of Rapes, Sex Trafficking Victims Posted to Site." The Daily Wire. https://www.dailywire.com/news/pornhub-under-fire-after-videos-of-rapes-sex-trafficking-victims-posted-to-site

Brown, Raymond E., Joseph A. Fitzmyer, and Roland E. Murphy, editors. *The New Jerome Biblical Commentary.* Englewood Cliffs, NJ: Prentice Hall, 1990.

Burke, Theresa Ph.D. "How Trauma Impacts the Brain." Rachel's Vineyard Ministries, https://rachelsvineyard.org/downloads/Canada%20Conference%2008/TextofBrainPP.pdf

Calvete, Esther. "Mental Health Characteristics of Men Who Abuse Their Intimate Partner." https://scielo.isciii.es/pdf/sanipe/v10n2/revision.pdf

Carnes, Patrick J., Ph.D. with Bonnie Phillips, Ph.D. *The Betrayal Bond: Breaking Free of Exploitive Relationships.* Deerfield Beach, FL: Health Communications, Inc., 2019.

Carter, Les, Ph.D. *Enough About You, Let's Talk About Me: How to Recognize & Manage the Narcissists in Your Life.* San Francisco, Ca: Jossey-Bass, A Wiley Imprint, 2005.

Carver, Joseph M. Ph.D., "Love and Stockholm Syndrome: The Mystery of Loving an Abuser." http://drjoecarver.makesweb-sites.com/clients/49355/File/love_and_stockholm_syn-drome.html

Catechism of the Catholic Church: With Modifications from the Editio Typica. 1994. Reprint, New York: Image Books/Doubleday, 1995.

Catherine of Siena. *The Dialogue.* Translated by Suzanne Noffke, O.P. Mahwah, NJ: Paulist Press, 1980.

Catherine of Siena. *The Letters of Catherine of Siena, Volume II.* Translated by Suzanne Noffke, O.P. Tempe, AZ: Arizona Center for Medieval and Renaissance Studies, 2001.

Catherine of Siena. *The Letters of Catherine of Siena, Volume IV.* Translated by Suzanne Noffke, O.P. Tempe, AZ: Arizona Center for Medieval and Renaissance Studies, 2008.

Catholic Exchange. "Actions Speak Louder Than Words." https://catholicexchange.com/actions-speak-louder-words

Catholic Online. "Thursday Homily: St. Anthony of Padua Reminds Us, Actions Speak Louder Than Words." https://www.catholic.org/homily/yearoffaith/story.php?id=51346

Dailymotion. "Mick Jagger Interview 1984." https://www.dailymotion.com/video/x18tmrl

Diocese of Raleigh, NC. "Freedom to Remarry: Procedures in the Diocese of Raleigh." https://dioceseofraleigh.org/sites/default/files/inline-files/Tribunal-brochure-2021-English.pdf

Domesticshelters.org. "Domestic Violence Statistics: The Hard Truth About Domestic Violence." https://www.domesticshelters.org/articles/statistics/domestic-violence-statistics

Douglas, J.D., editor. *The New Greek-English Interlinear New Testament*. Translated by Robert K. Brown and Philip W. Comfort. Carol Stream, IL: Tyndale House Publishers, Inc., 1990.

Duffy, Lisa. "Abusive Marriages & Divorce: What Does the Church Say?" CatholicMatch.com. https://plus.catholic-match.com/blog/2012/08/abusive-marriages-and-divorce-what-does-the-church-say/

Duffy, Lisa. *Mending the Heart: A Catholic Annulment Companion*. Huntington, IN: Our Sunday Visitor, Inc., 2018.

Dutton, Donald G. *The Abusive Personality: Violence and Control in Intimate Relationships, 2nd Edition*. NY, NY: The Guilford Press, 2007.

Dutton, Donald G. and Andrew J. Strazomski. "Borderline Personality in Perpetrators of Psychological and Physical Abuse" in *Violence and Victims, Vol. 8, No. 4*, 1993.

Enright, Robert Ph.D. *Forgiveness is a Choice: A Step-by-Step Process for Resolving Anger and Restoring Hope*. Washington, D.C.: American Psychological Association, 2001.

Enright, Robert Ph.D. *The Forgiving Life: A Pathway to Overcoming Resentment and Creating a Legacy of Love.* Washington, D.C.: American Psychological Association, 2014.

Enright, Robert Ph.D. "Is Forgiving for the Self or for the One Who Offended?" *Psychology Today.* https://www.psychologyto-day.com/us/blog/the-forgiving-life/201903/is-forgiving-the-self-or-the-one-who-offended

Evans, Patricia. *Verbal Abuse Survivors Speak Out: On Relationship and Recovery.* Avon, MA: Adams Media, 1993.

Evans, Patricia. *The Verbally Abusive Man: Can He Change?* Avon, MA: Adams Media, 2006.

Evans, Patricia. *The Verbally Abusive Relationship, Expanded Third Edition: How to Recognize it and How to Respond.* Avon, MA: Adams Media, 2010.

Forward, Susan Ph.D. *Emotional Blackmail: When the People in Your Life Use Fear, Obligation and Guilt to Manipulate You.* NY, NY: HarperCollins, 1997.

Forward, Susan Ph.D. *Men Who Hate Women & the Women Who Love Them.* NY, NY: Bantam Books, 2002.

Gilkerson, Luke. "Yes, Porn is Cheating. Here's Why." Covenant Eyes. https://www.covenanteyes.com/2015/01/19/ using-porn-is-cheating/

Gottman, John and Neil Jacobson. *When Men Batter Women: New Insights into Ending Abusive Relationships.* NY, NY: Simon& Schuster, 1998.

Hahn, Scott and Curtis Mitch, editors. *The Ignatius Catholic Study Bible, Revised Standard Version: Genesis.* San Francisco, Ca: Ignatius Press, 2010.

Hahn, Scott and Curtis Mitch, editors. *The Ignatius Catholic Study Bible, New Testament, Revised Standard Version, Second Catholic Edition.* San Francisco: Ignatius Press, 2010.

Hahn, Scott. *Signs of Life: 40 Catholic Customs and Their Biblical Roots.* NY, NY: Doubleday, 2009.

Halley, Dorothy and Steve. "Cracking the Code: Understanding the Different Motives of Those Who Batter." Online course, Family Peace Initiative. https://fpiacademy.thinkific.com/courses/cracking-the-code-understanding-the-different-motives-of-those-who-batter

Hamilton, Katherine. "Here's How Your Porn Habit Could Be Helping Human Sex Traffickers." NBC News. https://nbc-2.com/news/2021/01/12/heres-how-your-porn-habit-could-be-helping-human-sex-traffickers/

Hennessy, Don. *How He Gets Into Her Head: The Mind of the Male Intimate Abuser.* Cork, Ireland: Atrium, an imprint of Cork University Press, 2012.

Herman, Judith. *Trauma and Recovery: The Aftermath of Violence—From Domestic Abuse to Political Terror.* NY: Basic Books, 2015.

Hirigoyen, Marie-France. *Stalking the Soul: Emotional Abuse and the Erosion of Identity.* NY, NY: Helen Marx Books, 2004.

The Holy See. Code of Canon Law. http://www.vatican.va/archive/cod-iuris-canonici/eng/documents/cic_lib4-cann998-1165_en.html#CHAPTER_IX

Holzworth-Munroe, Amy and Gregory L. Stuart. "Typologies of Male Batterers: Three Subtypes and the Differences Among Them." https://psych.indiana.edu/documents/holzworth-munroe-and-stuart-1994.pdf

Holzworth-Munroe, Amy and Jeffrey C Meehan. "Typologies of Men Who are Maritally Violent: Scientific and Clinical

Implications." *Journal of interpersonal violence* vol. 19,12 (2004): 1369-89. https://pubmed.ncbi.nlm.nih.gov/15492053/ #affiliation-1

James, Austin. *Emotional Abuse, Silent Killer of Marriage: A 30-Year Abuser Speaks Out* (2016).

John Chrysostom. *"Homily on Ephesians:* Homily 20." *New Advent.* https://www.newadvent.org/fathers/230120.htm

John Paul II. *Evangelium Vitae (The Gospel of Life).* The Holy See. http://www.vatican.va/content/john-paul-ii/en/encyclicals/doc-uments/hf_jp-ii_enc_25031995_evangelium-vitae.pdf

John Paul II. *Familiaris Consortio.* The Holy See. https://www.vati-can.va/content/john-paul-ii/en/apost_exhortations/docu-ments/hf_jp-ii_exh_19811122_familiaris-consortio.html

John Paul II. *Man and Woman He Created Them: A Theology of the Body.* Translated by Michael Waldstein. Boston, MA: Pauline Books & Media, 2006.

John Paul II. "Message of the Holy Father to the Youth of the World on the Occasion of the XVI World Youth Day." The Holy See. https://www.vatican.va/content/john-paul-ii/en/messages/youth/documents/hf_jp-ii_mes_20010215_xvi-world-youth-day.html

John Paul II. *Mulieus Dignitatem (On the Dignity and Vocation of Women).* The Holy See. http://www.vatican.va/content/john-paul-ii/en/apost_letters/1988/documents/hf_jp-ii_apl_1988-0815_mulieris-dignitatem.html

Johnson, Michael P. and Kathleen J. Ferraro. "Research on Domestic Violence in the 1990s: Making Distinctions." Penn State Univer-sity. http://personal.psu.edu/mpj/2000%20JMF%20Johnson%20&%20Ferraro.pdf

Keener, Craig S. "Marriage Roles in Antiquity." In *NIV Cultural Backgrounds Study Bible: Bringing to Life the Ancient World of*

Scripture. Edited by Craig S. Keener and John H. Walton. Grand Rapids, MI: Zondervan, 2016.

Keener, Craig S. *Paul Women & Wives: Marriage and Women's Ministry in the Letters of Paul.* Peabody, MA: Hendrickson Publishers, Inc., 1992.

Kilcher, Jewel. *Never Broken: Songs are Only Half the Story.* NY, NY: Penguin Random House LLC, 2015.

Kowalska, Maria Faustina. *Diary of Saint Maria Faustina Kowalska.* Translated by Adam and Danuta Pasicki and Archbishop George Pearce, S.M. Stockbridge, MA: Association of Marian Helpers, 2012.

Leonard, Erin Ph.D. "Does a Narcissist Believe His or Her Own Lies?" Psychology Today. https://www.psychologytoday.com/us/blog/peaceful-parenting/201906/does-narcissist-believe-his-or-her-own-lies

Levine, Amy-Jill and Marc Zvi Brettler, editors. *The Jewish Annotated New Testament: Second Edition, NRSV.* NY: Oxford University Press, 2011.

Luben, Shelley. "Ex-Porn Star Tells the Truth about the Porn Industry." Covenant Eyes. https://www.covenanteyes.com/2008/10/28/ex-porn-star-tells-the-truth-about-the-porn-industry/

MacKenzie, Jackson. *Psychopath Free: Recovering from Emotionally Abusive Relationships with Narcissists, Sociopaths, and Other Toxic People (Expanded Edition).* NY, NY: Berkley Books, 2015.

Maxineau, Valerie JCL. "Annulment Basics." *National Association of Catholic Family Life Ministers*, Professional Development Webinar. https://nacflm.org. (June 17, 2021).

McKenna, Chris. "Porn-Induced Erectile Dysfunction: The Science, Stats, and Stories of PIED." Covenant Eyes, https://www.covenanteyes.com/2017/08/07/porn-induced-ed-science-stats-stories-pied/

John W. Miller. "Seeing How a Marriage Wasn't Meant to Be." Wall Street Journal. https://www.wsj.com/articles/seeing-how-a-marriage-wasnt-meant-to-be-1442531064

Moncher, Frank J. Ph.D. "Life Matters: Domestic Violence." United States Conference of Catholic Bishops. https://www.usccb.org/prolife/life-matters-domestic-violence

National Domestic Violence Hotline. "What is Gaslighting?" https://www.thehotline.org/resources/what-is-gaslighting/

Paul VI. *Humanae Vitae*. The Holy See. http://www.vatican.va/content/paul-vi/en/encyclicals/documents/hf_p-vi_enc_25071968_humanae-vitae.html

Peck, M. Scott M.D. *People of the Lie: The Hope for Healing Human Evil*. NY, NY: Touchstone, a division of Simon & Schuster, Inc., 1998.

Peterson, Eugene H. *Practice Resurrection: A Conversation on Growing Up in Christ*. Grand Rapids, MI: William B. Eerdmans Publishing Company, 2010.

Ramírez, Most Reverend Ricardo, C.S.B. "Speaking the Unspeakable: A Pastoral Letter on Domestic Violence." Accessed through the online course "Violence and Abuse in Catholic & Christian Families: Preparing an Effective and Compassionate Pastoral Response." Pax in Familia. https://health-transformations.learnworlds.com/course/ violence-and-abuse-in-catholic-and-christian-families

Raymond of Capua. *The Life of Catherine of Siena*. Translated by Conleth Kearns, O.P. Wilmington, DE: Michael Glazier, Inc., 1980.

Simon, George Jr., Ph.D. *In Sheep's Clothing: Understanding and Dealing with Manipulative People, Revised Edition*. Little Rock, AR: Parkhurst Brothers, Inc., 2010.

Sommer, Carl J. *We Look For a Kingdom: The Everyday Lives of the Early Christians.* San Francisco, CA: Ignatius Press, 2007.

Sri, Edward. "Anger and Virtue." https://www.catholiceducation.org/en/marriage-and-family/parenting/anger-and-virtue.html. Catholic Education Resource Center

Thomas Aquinas. *Summa Contra Gentiles, Book One: God.* Translated by Anton C. Pegis, F.R.S.C. Reprint, Notre Dame, IN: University of Notre Dame Press, 1975.

Thomas Aquinas. *Summa Theologica I.* Translated by the Fathers of the English Dominican Province. Reprint, Notre Dame, IN: Christian Classics, 1981.

Thomas Aquinas. *Summa Theologica I-II.* Translated by the Fathers of the English Dominican Province. Reprint, Notre Dame, IN: Christian Classics, 1981.

Trouvé, Marianne Lorraine, ed. *The Sixteen Documents of Vatican II.* Boston: Pauline Books & Media, 1999.

United States Conference of Catholic Bishops. "Catholic Response to Sexual and Domestic Violence and Abuse." https://www.usccb.org/issues-and-action/marriage-and-family/marriage/domestic-violence/upload/Catholic-Response-to-Sexual-and-Domestic-Violence-Report-Final.pdf

United States Conference of Catholic Bishops. "Life Matters: Domestic Violence." https://www.usccb.org/prolife/life-matters-domestic-violence

United States Conference of Catholic Bishops. "Marriage: Love and Life in the Divine Plan." https://www.usccb.org/resources/pastoral-letter-marriage-love-and-life-in-the-divine-plan.pdf

United States Conference of Catholic Bishops. "When I Call for Help." https://www.usccb.org/topics/marriage-and-family-life-ministries/when-i-call-help-pastoral-response-domestic-violence

Van der Kolk, Bessel, M.D. *The Body Keeps the Score.* NY, NY: Penguin Books, 2014.

van Maren, Jonathan. "40 Sex-Abuse Survivors Launch $40M Lawsuit Against Pornhub for Profiting from Illegal Vids." LifeSiteNews. https://www.lifesitenews.com/ blogs/40-sex-abuse-survivors-launch-40m-lawsuit-against-pornhub-for-profiting-from-illegal-vids/

Walker, Lenore E. *The Battered Woman.* NY, NY: William Morrow, An Imprint of HarperCollins, 1979.

Walker, Pete. *Complex PTSD: From Surviving to Thriving.* Lafayette, CA: An Azure Coyote Book, 2013.

Welland, Christauria, Psy.D. *How Can We Help to End Violence in Catholic Families? A Guide for Clergy, Religious and Laity.* Pax in Familia. http://paxinfamilia.org/wp-content/uploads/2019/07/How-can-we-help-to-end-violence-2nd-edition.pdf

Welland, Christauria, Psy.D. "Motivating the Person Who Uses Abuse and Violence to Seek Healing." Catholic University Symposium. http://www.catholicsforfamilypeace.org/uploads/9/7/5/4/9754767/cua_symposium_716_motivating_abusers_for_tx_integrated_final.pdf

Welland, Christauria, Psy.D. "Violence and Abuse in Catholic & Christian Families: Preparing an Effective and Compassionate Pastoral Response." Online course, Pax in Familia. https://health-transformations.learnworlds.com/course/violence-and-abuse-in-catholic-and-christian-families

Wexler, David B., Ph.D. *When Good Men Behave Badly.* Oakland, CA: New Harbinger Publications, Inc., 2004.

Wilson, Gary. "Brain Studies on Porn Users & Sex Addicts." Your Brain on Porn. https://www.yourbrainonporn.com/relevant-research-and-articles-about-the-studies/brain-studies-on-porn-users-sex-addicts/#brain

Gary Wilson. "Sexual Problems." Your Brain on Porn,
    https://www.yourbrainonporn.com/sexual-problems/
World Health Organization. "Violence Against Women."
    https://www.who.int/news-room/fact-sheets/detail/violence-
    against-women